I dedicate this book to all the staff that are working, and have worked, at Ekstedt. The success of the restaurant is all thanks to you.

You are the best!

Niklas Ekstedt

EKSTEDT

The Nordic art of analogue cooking

BLOOMSBURY ABSOLUTE

LONDON · OXFORD · NEW YORK · NEW DELHI · SYDNEY

Contents

Introduction

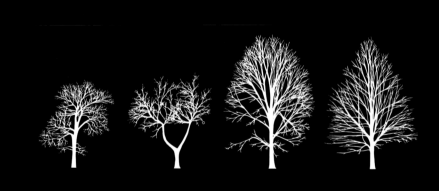

From Niklas

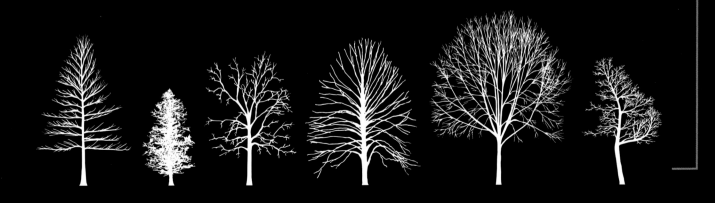

Fire – the heart & soul of Nordic cuisine

The year before Ekstedt opened was a bewildering and overwhelming time for me. Our eldest son had just been born – the greatest thing that ever happened to me, until I became a father of two wonderful boys – and I was, of course, on cloud nine. But at the same time, I had experienced a rough year professionally. Although highly acclaimed and popular, I had decided to close down my fine-dining restaurant in Helsingborg (a small coastal city in Skåne, the southern-most province in Sweden), and the opening of a new restaurant in Stockholm hadn't gone according to plan. Meanwhile, things seemed to be going incredibly well for all my friends and colleagues. Chefs and sous-chefs previously working for me had come to open their own restaurants and were now highly praised for their take on the New Nordic Food Manifesto, with restaurants such as NoMa and Fäviken, and chefs like Daniel Berlin, leading the way. The feeling of being an up-and-coming artist peeping behind the curtain ready to get on stage to perform my magic, turned into an unbearable disorientation and loneliness. I had been part of something new and ambitious, but while my fellow chefs went on to dominate world gastronomy, I became a mere observer. I remember finding myself at a crossroads not knowing which direction to take; was pursuing my dream really worth all the hard work and long hours away from my family? Perhaps it was time for me to leave the restaurant life for good and do something completely different.

My wife and I had recently bought a summer cottage on Ingarö, in the beautiful Stockholm archipelago, where we had created a really nice kitchen. However, since we hadn't had a chance to fix all the plumbing and rewire the old electricity, the kitchen lacked running water, and I preferred to cook out on the patio. I began to experiment with outdoor cooking and soon made a simple firepit out of an old Weber charcoal barbecue lid turned upside down, putting a cast-iron pan in the flames. The stronger my curiosity for open-fire cooking grew, the more soiled and sootier our patio became. But I loved it.

Nonetheless, my endeavour made me wonder why Nordic kitchens hadn't stayed true to their roots and why we had abandoned our conventional cooking techniques in favour of more contemporary ways of cooking. Whilst many other cuisines around the world – the Italian and their famous Neapolitan wood-fired pizza, for example – remain faithful to their traditional cooking techniques, and instead refine and learn how to master the raw materials to attain a neo-gastronomic sophistication, Sweden, as well as the other Nordic countries, had chosen a different path. Among Swedes, our traditional cooking techniques are long forgotten, and all that remains are scanty relics displayed in open-air museums. When electricity was introduced in Swedish homes a century ago, we quickly became accustomed to the new way of cooking. But when discarding grandma's old stove and wood burner, we didn't only throw away the trusty cast-iron pans and waffle irons to make room for induction cookers, convection ovens and halogen light bulbs; more importantly we threw out old family recipes, as well as the knowledge of the original and unique way to cook many of the dishes. This choice fascinated me, as I lit the logs in my summer cottage fire pit and contemplated my future.

A few weeks later I went back to Stockholm and the grand National Library of Sweden, where I read every book I could find about ancient Swedish cooking techniques and methods. Fairly soon, I realised that everything associated with traditional Nordic cuisine was invented before electricity became an essential part of our everyday life, and our gastronomic heritage still revolved around a wood stove or a large fireplace. Traditionally, a large cauldron over an open fire was the heart of every home and kitchen. For the rich as well as for the poor, the fire and the wood itself was of the greatest importance to the family, since it wasn't only used for cooking but also for heating (hence our love for snuggling up in front of the fireplace – today perhaps more commonly known due to the Danish word *hygge*). If you ran out of wood, or for other reasons couldn't keep the fire burning, your house immediately turned cold and damp, especially during the long, dark winter months. To spend the autumn stacking wood to make sure you had a pile of logs to last the winter became a matter of life and death. And consequently, cooking was determined by how much wood you had piled up. When reading this, the pieces of my gastronomic jigsaw puzzle fell into place, and for the first time I fully realised the magnitude of the role which birch wood played in the Nordic culture. At the same time, I was saddened by the thought that the fire once keeping us alive had been degraded to something that today was only used to create a cosy ambience in Swedish sitting rooms.

This made me want to experiment a bit more and I decided to cook exclusively with birch wood, if only just to try and see where it would take me as a chef. When returning to Ingarö I built a proper fireplace and a larger fire pit, bought tons of cast-iron pans, waffle irons and griddles in various sizes and set out on my mission. Meanwhile, a restaurant venue in central Stockholm came on the market, and one of my friends, Vimal Kovac – who ran one of the more prominent restaurant groups in Stockholm – was quick to get his hands on it. The premises were small, but the location was to die for. When Vimal, not knowing the extent of my current passion, told me the restaurant had housed a wood-fired pizzeria, a flickering flame rose in my chest. Standing with sooty hands and heart pounding so loudly I could barely hear myself think, overlooking this enormous pile of birch wood in my backyard, I knew this wasn't just an opportunity; it was a message. I should open a restaurant using nothing but traditional open-fire cooking techniques.

Andreaz Norén, another friend of mine, had been at a catering school in Åre in Sweden, where he'd met a chef named Gustav Otterberg. Gustav was as passionate as me about open-fire cooking and spent most of his time in the forest with friends and family – and had moreover single-handedly built a terrific fireplace at home. A few days later we met in downtown Stockholm and did what I think many people before us have done when struck by an idea too unique to ignore; we used the restaurant napkin to clarify our vision. We sketched and talked, and for many hours discussed the heart and soul of Swedish gastronomy and what the two of us could do to turn old techniques into something contemporary, as well as how to convert thought into action and how to make it work in a restaurant atmosphere. Gustav's ideas were brilliant and many of the

16

things we designed on the napkin that afternoon are methods we still use in Ekstedt today.

A few months after that first meeting Gustav came to be the restaurant's first ever chef, and we worked closely, side by side, for the first year. I can honestly say that much of the restaurant's fame and glory is owing to Gustav's skills and craftsmanship, and his daring creativity. If it weren't for him, Ekstedt wouldn't be the restaurant it is today. In the end, sadly, Gustav decided he needed to move on, since he was finding it more and more difficult to combine restaurant hours with family life. I completely respect his decision – being a family man myself – but I can't help but miss our time together in the kitchen; after the restaurant had closed for the evening we used to sit down and, on napkins that with time had turned into proper sketchpads, jot down thoughts and visions for how to further evolve and expand our menu.

Within six months from the first phone call from Vimal, my new restaurant began to take shape. A friend of mine had earlier mentioned an architect, Jeanette Dalrot, who just recently had designed an acclaimed restaurant in Stockholm Old Town – called Djuret – and was keen to take on a new project. I told her about my ideas for the decor. For me, personally, it was important that not only the menu but the entire restaurant, interior and all, reflected my childhood in Järpen, a small village in northern Sweden, as well as all the summers I've spent in Skåne. The result was a black and white half-timbered wall, a homage to the traditional picturesque Scanian architecture, on the left hand side of the restaurant, and a massive wood oven facing the dining area, as a reminder to myself and my guests of the very foundation on which Swedish culinary culture is built, and in which we once baked our daily bread.

The first few months after the opening were far from the joy that running Ekstedt is today. No one seemed to understand what we were trying to do or what I wanted to achieve. The reviews were mainly about me having opened a new barbecue restaurant. Luckily, a British food critic, who since sadly has passed away, had a guest column in the Swedish newspaper *Dagens Nyheter* at the time and was visiting Stockholm to write about the latest entries on the capital's gastronomic scene. He honoured Ekstedt with a beautifully written piece, where he managed to communicate exactly what we were doing, in a way that I myself had failed to explain to the media, and for which I'm ever so grateful. His name was A. A. Gill, and being reviewed by an internationally recognised food critic opened the floodgates to Swedish food critics as well as guests, giving us top reviews in the three most important national papers. All of a sudden, the restaurant was fully booked weekends in advance, and the great challenge quickly shifted to keeping up the high-level gastronomy and getting the plates out in time without cheating and using electricity.

I like to compare my restaurant to Kon-Tiki – the raft built by the Norwegian explorer Thor Heyerdahl in 1947, following ancient Polynesian technology, for an expedition across the Pacific Ocean. Ekstedt wasn't just a restaurant among others but as much a historic experiment; was it at all possible to use old cooking techniques in a contemporary way and, equally important, would it suffice to compete with the high-end restaurants in

Stockholm? As it turned out, it worked rather well – actually *really* well – once we had found not only our feet, but the ingredients needed to deliver the high-class gastronomy we wanted to attain. We soon came to realise that we couldn't use the raw materials one would usually go for in a neo-Nordic restaurant – anything small, fragile, light, neat or dainty had to make room for heavy, thick, coarse raw materials that were much better suited for the high temperatures in our kitchen. But this knowledge was crucial for our boat to float – and honestly, it didn't just float, it sailed majestically – and the food we served turned out to be something completely different to anything Stockholm had ever tasted before. And all due to something so basic and primal as firewood.

When we, after our first year, were awarded with a Guide Michelin star, I was told that Ekstedt was one of the few Michelin starred-restaurants not using electricity. This was something I hadn't even reflected on; I had been so focused on serving anything at all without a cooker, that the mere thought of being awarded a star for my mission never crossed my mind. But my low expectations and the buzz when the unexpected eventually happened, made Ekstedt an immediate international success, and the waiting list grew longer and longer. I, on the other hand, stuck to the same paved path I had started on, and was determined not to take any shortcuts, however convenient, or to give in and install an electric cooker. So far, I have kept my promise and stayed true to my initial idea, and even today the traditional analogue way of cooking is the mantra in our gastronomy. (But I have a confession to make; lately we have cheated a bit by using charcoal, which, when opening, was something I said I would never do. However, I've come to like it – more and more, actually – and to be quite honest with you, well-made charcoal is extremely nice to work with, especially in a fireplace the size as the ones at Ekstedt.)

Niklas Ekstedt
Stockholm, 2020

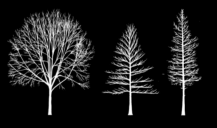

Tools & Techniques

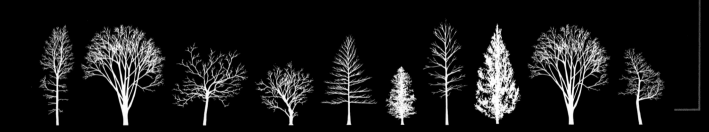

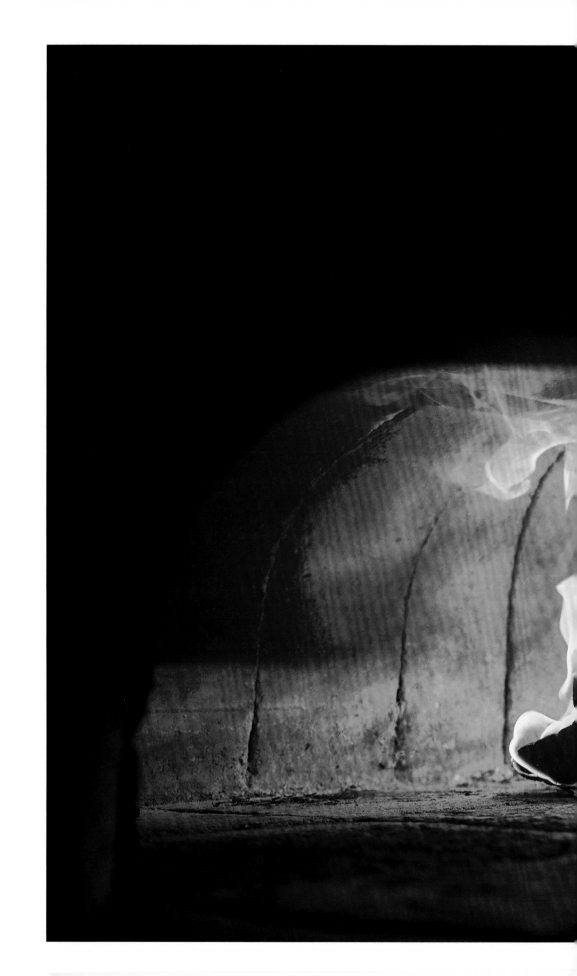

Wood oven

22

The wood-fired oven is the heart of the Ekstedt kitchen. Everything happens in and around it. Even though the fire dies for a few hours now and then, the heat never does. The oven is working every day of the year, all around the clock.

The oven at Ekstedt is of the Roman type – the oldest type there is. The style is old-fashioned with a rounded ceiling. The flat bottom part is made of bricks covered with clay. That flat surface is sometimes used to bake flatbreads but most of the time it is just used as a 'normal' oven, for baking sourdough bread and cakes or for cooking vegetables overnight in the residual heat from the previous night's service.

We light up the oven at 8 o'clock in the morning. At that hour it is still quite hot from the night before, around 80–100°C. So we re-fire it and bring it up to 500°C. The oven is fuelled with burning birch wood and we usually use six–eight logs to start with to work up the heat, which takes around two hours. Usually it is the same person working with the oven throughout the whole process. There is no thermometer but we have a couple of ways of measuring the heat. One way is to watch the bricks: as the heat slowly spreads from the back of the oven to the front, it makes the bricks turn from dark to light. We count the bricks that have turned light – every one means 50°C more heat. When all the bricks inside have turned from dark grey/black to white, there is enough heat for us to work.

When the oven is hot enough we let the flame slowly die, then spread out the embers to create a bed on which we drop the vegetables we want to prepare ahead for the evening. So the first use of the wood oven is the heat from the embers. Burnt leek is one of the things we often make at this point as it is part of one of our signature dishes.

After that we move on to the salt-baked vegetables. We fill a gastro tray with sea salt and add vegetables, then set it on the spread-out embers. The embers conduct the heat to the salt and from the salt to the vegetables. Most root vegetables – beetroot, turnips, carrots and so on – can be cooked like this, with salt helping to dry out the vegetables and concentrate the flavour. When the embers die, at around 11 o'clock in the morning, we clean the oven to make it ready for baking bread.

Using an ember scraper, we collect all the embers together in the oven. Then we wrap a wet towel around the scraper and, with a bucket of water at room temperature, use it to clean the oven. The wet cloth takes away the ashes, and also adds humidity to the stone, which is crucial for baking bread. After this, the temperature will be around 300°C. We close the oven door and the ventilation trap, then leave it to rest for 30 minutes. During this time the moisture builds up and the heat evens out in the oven.

By noon the oven is around 270°C and is at the perfect condition for us to use the wooden shovel to get the bread into the oven, where it bakes for about 30 minutes.

Once the bread is done we re-light the oven for the afternoon preparation, and it becomes a pastry oven. We bake the cakes for the service in the evening – almond cake or buckwheat cake, for instance – and 'kaffegodis' (coffee candy). At 4 o'clock we clean the oven again, this time with a rounded metal brush, just a brief cleaning before service.

The service oven is kept at 300°C, so that we can bake the occasional flatbread and sear some meat, fish or vegetables in a pan in it, just like in an ordinary oven.

The final step is taken before we go home for the night. When the fire is dying and there are only a few embers glowing, we put vegetables that we want to slow cook during the night into the oven, whole white cabbage for example. Or we make stock by putting bones, vegetables and herbs in a big gastro tray, sealing it and sliding it into the oven where it can simmer gently all night – until the fire is lit the next morning, and the whole beautiful process starts over again.

Smoked

At Ekstedt we use two methods of smoking: cold smoke and hot smoke.

Cold smoke

The cold smoke is just for flavour and not for cooking. To get a cold smoke we select a piece of wood from the fire that is nearly burned out, and is smoking the most. We put it in the bottom compartment of the smoker and close the lid to get rid of the oxygen. When the smoke comes up through the three chimneys, it is cool. Sometimes we put a big box on top of the chimneys and cold smoke there, which is how we smoke butter, oil, fish, cheese or dried meat. But we can also use a chinois or a sieve on top of the fire, using a branch of juniper or hay to create the smoke, if we want to smoke something small during service.

Birch wood is the main fuel we use for the smoker, chosen for several reasons: it is a common tree in Sweden, and very sustainable; it is not very dense, so it has a fast flame and dies into embers quite quickly; and it has a good neutral smoke that gives the best smoky flavour.

Hot smoke

For hot smoking we add more heat by putting in
burning logs and embers to heat up the smoker.
Smoke could be seasoned by wet juniper branches
or blackcurrant branches, for example.

In the smoker we put a tray of whatever we want
to hot smoke – mainly fish, for example cod or pike-
perch). The temperature in the box is around 100°C
and a portion of fish will take 5–10 minutes to hot
smoke in there.

Hot smoking can be done to prepare food in
advance so it can be stored, but at Ekstedt the hot
smoke is normally used as a cooking tool during
service.

Ember

When you burn wood it turns into embers. While the embers are still glowing hot they can be used to cook or flavour almost any fresh ingredients, such as meat, fish, seafood or vegetables. As with flame-cooking, the outside of the food turns black.

At Ekstedt we use ember cooking as a cooking process for vegetables, which are put straight into the embers, or for searing meat and fish on top of the embers, or for infusing the embers in a liquid such as cream (see page 286 for the charcoal cream).

When we use ember cooking for vegetables, such as potatoes or Jerusalem artichokes, we put them straight into the embers to add a deeper flavour. After they've cooked all the way through, for about 30–45 minutes, we let them cool slightly before brushing off the ash.

Meat and fish are also great to cook with embers. We use this mainly as a way of seasoning the food, and so it's not cooked for long periods of time in this way.

If you try it at home, make sure to dry the surface of your chosen ingredients with a clean tea towel before placing them in the embers.

Hay-flamed

At Ekstedt we normally use a combination of techniques to make a dish, with hay flames often the final touch when preparing a dish during service. Covering ingredients with dry hay and setting it on fire gives a delicate taste of burnt hay and ash to the dish.

The space for hay-flaming is constructed of bricks and has a bottom layer of embers to provide heat. We drop hay on the embers, then place the food either directly on the hay or on a grill just above: shellfish such as scallops, or a whole fillet of salmon without the skin, can be put directly on the hay flames. When we want to sear and give flavour to beef we can either use the grill above or let the meat stay in the flames for a short while and then serve it directly.

Another way we use hay-flaming is to collect the ashes and blend them with sea salt to make hay salt, which we use for a last-minute seasoning.

Open fire

30

When we flame-cook vegetables we want them to be in direct contact with the flames, maybe 10–20cm above the burning birchwood fire. Flame-cooking is part of the morning preparation. Later, the flame-cooked vegetables are reheated in a pan or in the oven during service. We use the technique mainly for root vegetables such as swede, celeriac, turnips, carrots, parsnips, kohlrabi and so on.

So we make a fire. When it is burning, we place the whole vegetables directly in the flames to cook for 45–50 minutes, depending on size. This is a good way to cook vegetables as it really brings out the best in them, making them soft and very tasty (if you boil vegetables you lose a lot of the flavour).

The process can be thought of as a sort of sous-vide technique. The outside of the vegetable gets all black, but we only use the heart that has been properly cooked. A big celeriac could take one to two hours to flame-cook, then it needs to rest for half of the time it was cooked. When it reaches room temperature you can peel off the burnt skin to reveal the inside, which will have the most beautiful flavour.

Flambadou

The flambadou technique originated in the Basque country, between France and Spain, in the twelfth century, but we have also found recipes in old Swedish cookery books where the technique was used, albeit in a slightly different way. In those early days the hot fat was collected from under the rotisserie.

Basically flambadou cooking at Ekstedt means cooking by basting with burning fat. A piece of beef fat is placed in a red-hot cast-iron cone on a stick. The fat starts to burn because of the heat and is dripped down over the food being cooked.

The forged cast-iron tool itself is called a flambadou. The flambadou station is lit up some time before service. We cover the cast-iron cone with embers and leave it for around an hour until it is red hot – when the heat reaches 600°C.

You can flambadou any vegetable or meat (as is often done in France), but at Ekstedt we usually use the technique for fish and shellfish. Flambadou oysters is a favourite. The oysters are placed on a heavy metal tray. Then we put a piece of beef fat in the red-hot cone. As soon as the fat starts to flame and melt, the cone is held over the oysters so the burning fat drips on to them. It is a very fast cooking process, taking only a few seconds.

The beef fat we use comes from the dry-aged dairy cow meat we use in the kitchen; the beef has a lot of flavour with a nice marbling of fat. On the menu the beef cut we serve is entrecote, and when boning the beef we carve out the fat and collect it for the flambadou.

Cast-iron stove

34

Sweden has a long history of cast-iron production so it is no surprise that many of the tools traditionally used for cooking were made of cast iron. Cast-iron stoves rose in popularity in Sweden around 1850, and they often replaced open fires in the kitchen, or were sometimes installed in addition to the traditional open fire. The stoves were more effective at retaining heat and used less wood.

The stove at Ekstedt, which can be seen here, is estimated to be around 120 years old. We bought it from a private home in the Swedish archipelago, to be renovated, and it's been in use ever since.

Tools

36

The cast-iron utensils that are traditionally used in Nordic cooking are built to last, and it's not uncommon for pans to be handed down through the generations.

Cast-iron pans are very solid and retain their heat, even when something cold has been added to them, unlike other, more commonly used kitchen pans, and this is just one of the reasons they are so widely used in the kitchen at Ekstedt.

Some of the pans that we use are custom-made for us, but they are mostly purchased from Skeppshult, a traditional Swedish company established in 1906.

Flambadou, seen here on the right, are traditionally used in southern France and are known as *flamboir à lard*. This cast iron or steel cone is used to heat fat and butter, and you hang it above your fire so that it slowly drips down onto the ingredients (see page 32 for more on flambadou cooking).

Each day at Ekstedt we get through a lot of wood, especially birch, and it is all chopped by the restaurant team using our trusty axe.

The tools which can be seen in the image on the far right include the brushes and scraper for cleaning the oven each day. The oven should only be cleaned dry; we never use water to do this. Also shown are the paddle used to move bread in and out of the oven and the tongs used for grabbing hot pans or trays from out of the oven.

Autumn / Winter

With the Sami

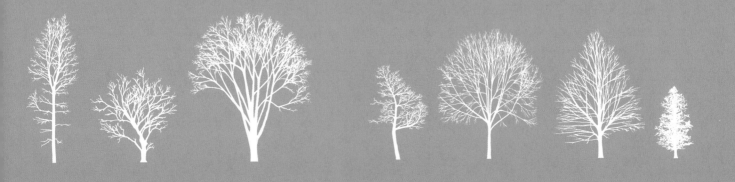

Herding the reindeer

46

Reindeer meat is fantastic in many ways, and I'm not the only Michelin-starred chef who considers it the highest quality. The reindeer are allowed to grow slowly while grazing on mountain slopes and drinking crystal clear water from rippling mountain brooks – in an all-natural environment free from antibiotics and artificial nutrition agents. They live out on the mountain slopes as much as possible but are moved between different seasonal pastures. During the summer months, when the reindeer are growing, they graze on protein-rich food such as grass, herbs and fungi in the mountains and forest. During the winter, they graze on energy-rich lichen. Every autumn the reindeer are herded down towards the forest areas, mainly because the temperature is falling and the reindeer need to find food. These photos were taken on such an occasion.

When the reindeer are brought down from the summer pastures, it's an opportunity to brand the livestock to identify the owner. Since reindeer calves born in spring and summer haven't yet been branded, the Sami families now make sure that each calf next to its mother is caught with a lasso and has the family's distinct mark cut into its ears. The annual slaughter also takes place while gathering the reindeer for winter. Reindeer husbandry is in many ways a sustainable livelihood and only a certain number of well-selected animals are slaughtered. It's important to ensure the slaughter doesn't interfere too much with the herd and to take no more than the animals needed.

Reindeer herding is part of a culture that our modern society knows very little about. Even Swedes who live close to the Sami have embarrassingly little knowledge about reindeer keepers, what they actually do and the advantages of reindeer meat. Reindeer herding is a brilliant example of how to make use of high-quality meat. The slaughter is as harmonious as a slaughter can be, and considerably calmer than any cattle, pigs or chickens will ever experience in the vast meat industry of today. Unfortunately, reindeer husbandry is threatened by global warming, cultural changes and mining and territorial conflicts. I think it's incredibly important for the Sami to be allowed to live the way they've always lived and I believe we all have a responsibility for preserving their livelihood – the reindeer – by making use of as much of the livestock as possible.

Within Sami culture the reindeer carries a strong symbolic value, and so it is not only the meat that is used; other parts of the animal, such as the skin and antlers, are used for clothing and art.

The Sami

48   Sami cooking and Sami cooking techniques have always had a special
place in my heart and are of great importance to me. I first got acquainted
with the Sami culture as a boy, when in the early 1970s my parents moved
to Jämtland (a municipal region in Norrland, the most northern part of
Sweden). At the time, the village Järpen, where I was born, had a Sami
boarding school, and although my parents weren't Sami themselves, their
curiosity about the Sami culture had a major impact on our family. From
an early age, Sami food and traditions became a part of my everyday life,
and my fascination for this natural way of living grew stronger when
I began to cook. Apart from picking blueberries, lingonberries and
mushrooms, my parents took part in the reindeer slaughter every autumn,
and as a treat we would have fresh reindeer meat at home. Just recently
my mother told me that when the Sami boarding school closed down,
my parents bought a few of the beds from the dormitory for me and my
siblings to sleep in. Perhaps that's why I've always felt a connection to the
Sami – and still do – and why I'm so keen on protecting the Sami heritage.

    Many years later, when I started Ekstedt, I knew from deep within
that open-fire cooking and cast iron were the way for me to go, and
unsurprisingly I bought reindeer meat, char and trout from Sami families
up north. Not only is this meat suitable for my way of cooking, for me
there's also a lot of nostalgia in the whole process of preparing and cooking
with traditional Sami techniques.

The reindeer gathering

50

To be part of the annual reindeer gathering is an extraordinary treat, to say the least, and something I'm very grateful to have experienced. The reindeer run clockwise, around and around, within large enclosures. Around this massive circle of reindeer, the different Sami families gather to spot and brand their calves. The reindeer are caught with a lasso and held to the ground while carefully branded with the family's unique marking. The Sami traditionally brand their animals this way, since the reindeer ears have little sensation.

The reindeer gathering is not only a practical event, but also an opportunity for the different Sami families to get together. During most of the year everyone works in different areas or locations, hence this ceremony's importance for exchanging recent experiences or for discussing problems or adversities that may have occurred during the past year. It's often a very warm and joyous occasion, and it's nice to see so many of the Sami families together at once; many are related or have known each other for a long time. At night there's usually a great campfire where everyone talks about past and present times and how to solve issues of importance to the Sami today.

The reindeer meat

With the Sami
Autumn / Winter

Most of the reindeer meat is cut and sent off to various refiners, where it's smoked or turned into products for the Sami to resell. The meat that's not suitable for smoking or other refinement is thinly sliced, frozen and turned into sautéed reindeer (known as *renskav* in Swedish). This is a very popular dish, especially in the northern part of Scandinavia, and is often served in school canteens. 'Norrland's national dish', it is basically quickly fried meat, onion, garlic and a splash of cream served with mashed potatoes.

I have many fond memories from Norrland, and one of my favourite dishes originates there. *Maträttens samiska namn här* is one of those slightly unusual dishes you either love or hate – but if you love it, you really love it. One part of the reindeer that's often left over when everything else has been taken care of is the femur. The leg in all its simplicity is placed over an open fire for the bone marrow to cook. When done, you use the handle on your knife to carefully 'knock' the boiled marrow out of the bone. Served with bleak roe (löjrom) the contrast between the salty and the fat makes for a real delicacy – for some, that is. But I love it! It feels like something we've been eating since ancient times, and archaeological findings actually show how our ancestors put entire bones in the flames before digging into the lovely, fat bone marrow.

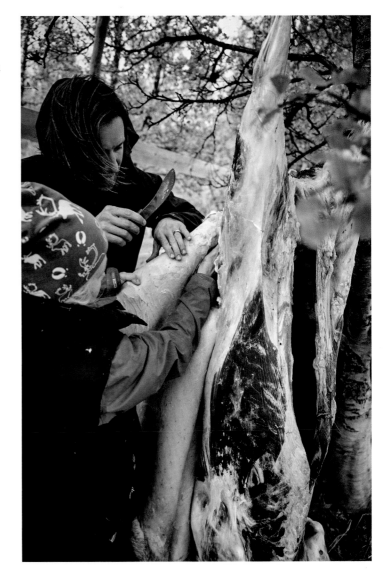

Cooking with the Sami

56

Another delicacy that I've been served several times during my stay with the Sami – most recently by Andreas (in the photos on pages 49 and 60) – is pancakes made from reindeer blood. Fresh reindeer blood is lightly whisked with rye flour, syrup and an egg, then fried in a special cast iron griddle with some butter and served with sour cream and lingonberry. It sounds rather barbaric but is actually heaven on a plate – especially when eaten in such beautiful surroundings!

Quite a few of the cooking methods and techniques I've learnt to master and actually practise in Ekstedt today, I've picked up from the Sami. All of them are about going back to basics and keeping it simple. The Sami food culture and their way of living is in many ways thrifty and sustainable; everything is made useful, in one way or another, and very little is thrown away. In the great challenge the Western world faces today – of making use of more and throwing away less – the Sami way of living is a brilliant example of how to live more responsibly and in harmony with nature. One can't help noticing that Sami families show a greater respect for the environment and their livestock, and a greater love for the natural raw materials and the food that ends up on their plates, than most of us do.

The reindeer are a natural part of the Sami life, and although the livestock is brought up to be slaughtered, the Sami show an enormous and admirable respect and love for their animals; not only due to the reindeer being their livelihood, but mainly because reindeer husbandry is an important part of Sami culture and tradition and therefore needs to be well cared for. The game and reindeer meat are consequently treated with respect and carefully prepared and cooked to make sure nothing goes to waste. This is clearly evident in the techniques they use, and for a chef this respectful way of cooking is wonderful to see. Many of the traditional Sami cooking methods – such as hot-, cold- and juniper-smoking – are an important part of Ekstedt – and even to me personally – and I'm ever so grateful for having been part of the ancient Sami traditions and experiences.

Wood Oven

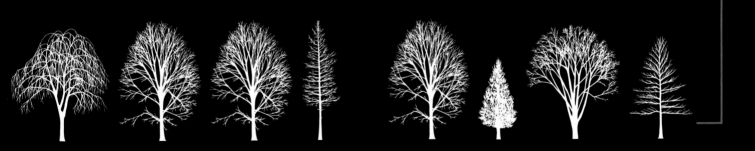

Flatbread, smoked moose heart & allspice

Wood Oven
Autumn / Winter

We serve this rye flatbread freshly baked from the wood oven, placing it on
the table with a smoking-hot cast-iron pan on the side to lightly sear the moose
heart in allspice butter with mushrooms and fresh tart lingonberries. It gives off
a beautiful aroma that surrounds the table.

**Serves 4 as a middle
course or snack**

200g moose heart
6–8 champignon mushrooms
1 tablespoon chopped parsley
50g lingonberries (page 288)
a bunch of chervil, bull's
    blood (beetroot leaf) and
    pea shoots, to garnish
sea salt

For the allspice butter
5 allspice berries
20g Smoked Butter (page
    285), at room temperature
70g unsalted butter, at room
    temperature
10ml sherry vinegar

For the flatbreads
150ml milk
30g butter
14g honey
5g fresh yeast
100g rye flour
100g strong wheat flour

To make the allspice butter, crush the allspice berries in a mortar and
pestle until finely ground. Combine with the smoked butter, unsalted
butter, sherry vinegar and 10g salt in a bowl and whisk until smooth
and evenly combined. Set aside at room temperature.

Trim the moose heart and cut into 5mm dice. Cold smoke for 5 minutes.
Leave at room temperature.

Clean the mushrooms, then grate roughly. Combine with 2 tablespoons
water in a pan and place over a medium-high heat. Simmer until all the
liquid has evaporated. Remove from the heat, season with salt and set aside.

For the flatbreads, mix together the milk, butter and honey in a pan. Heat
to 37°C. Pour the mixture into a large bowl, add the yeast and whisk to
dissolve. Add the flours and mix with the liquid into a dough, then knead
until smooth and shiny. Leave to rise, covered, in a warm place for about
45 minutes until doubled in size.

Preheat the oven to 225°C. If you have a baking stone, put it into the oven
to heat up, or heat up a baking tray. At the same time, put 4 individual
cast-iron pans, or 1 large cast-iron pan, in the oven to heat for 30 minutes
or until heated to 230°C (we check the temperature of the pans with a
laser thermometer).

Knock back the dough, then divide into 4 portions. Roll out each piece
of dough on a floured surface into an 8cm round. Bake on the hot baking
stone or baking tray for 3–4 minutes until puffed up and golden brown.

Meanwhile, assemble 4 cups with the ingredients in layers, starting with
mushrooms, then parsley, diced moose heart and lingonberries. Top each
with a quenelle of allspice butter. Alternatively, layer the ingredients in one
large serving dish.

At the table, add the allspice butter to the hot pan(s) and stir with a spoon
until melted, then add all the other ingredients in the cup or dish and sauté
for 1 minute, stirring. Serve with the freshly baked flatbreads topped with
the herbs.

Wild duck confit & overnight-baked cabbage

At the end of an evening's service, with the wood oven still warm, we use the remaining heat for overnight baking. Cooking a whole cabbage for a long time in a slowly decreasing temperature in the wood oven results in an almost sweet and caramelised taste. Poaching the wild duck leg in duck fat gives a deep flavour which works beautifully with the acidic element of pickled young spruce shoots.

Serves 4 as a main course

*For the overnight-baked
   cabbage*
1 white cabbage
butter, for searing

For the wild duck confit
4 wild duck legs
400ml duck fat
3 bay leaves
5 black peppercorns
sea salt

For the wild duck jus
1kg wild duck carcasses, skin
   and fat removed
2 celery sticks
1 large onion, cut in half
2 medium carrots, cut in half
200ml red wine
2.5 litres Chicken Stock (page
   279)
2 bay leaves
3 sprigs of thyme
5 black peppercorns
sea salt

For the pickled spruce shoots
100g sugar
50ml ättika (page 288)
½ teaspoon sea salt
200ml spruce shoots

For the butter-fried parsley
about 3 tablespoons Clarified
   Butter (page 284)
8 parsley leaves
sea salt

Preheat the oven to 150°C.

If necessary, trim the core of the cabbage to make a flat base, then set it on a baking tray and cook in the oven for 10–12 hours until soft in the centre. Remove from the oven and set aside to cool for 1 hour.

Season the duck legs with salt. Put them in a pan and cover with the duck fat. Add the bay leaves and peppercorns. Heat up to 82°C and keep at this temperature for 3–4 hours until the meat is coming away from the bone. Remove from the heat and cool down to around 50°C. Lift the duck legs from the fat and leave to drain. (If made ahead, keep in the fridge and heat up slowly for serving.)

Heat the oven to 220°C. Roast the duck carcasses in a baking tray in the oven until golden brown. Transfer the bones to a stockpot. Put the celery, onion and carrot in the baking tray and roast until golden brown, then add to the stockpot. Drain the fat from the baking tray and deglaze with the red wine. Bring to the boil, then pour the wine into the stockpot along with the chicken stock. Add the herbs and peppercorns. Bring to the boil, skimming off any scum that comes to the surface. Simmer for about 4 hours. Remove from the heat and let sit for 1 hour. Strain into a clean pan and reduce until you have 200–300ml of jus. Season with salt.

To pickle the spruce shoots, combine the sugar, ättika, salt and 150ml water in a saucepan. Bring to the boil over a medium-high heat, whisking to dissolve the sugar. Lower the heat, add the spruce shoots and simmer for 10 minutes. Leave to cool. (This keeps in the fridge for 1 month.)

For the butter-fried parsley, heat enough clarified butter in a wide pan to make a thin layer on the bottom. Carefully place the parsley leaves flat in the pan and sear over a medium heat for about 1 minute on each side until crispy. Drain on kitchen paper and sprinkle with salt.

Cut 4 slices from the overnight-baked cabbage (keep the rest in the fridge for up to 3 days) and sear in butter on both sides. Put the confit duck legs, skin side down, in another pan, heat up and sear over a medium heat.

Top the duck legs with pickled spruce shoots and garnish with butter-fried parsley. Serve with the seared cabbage and reheated duck jus.

Bone marrow toast with burnt hay salt

Wood Oven
Autumn / Winter

72

Roasting bone marrow in the wood oven gives off a deep, fatty, rich aroma. To add flavours from the fire, we burn hay and combine it with salt. After you set the hay on fire, make sure it all burns out – easily done if you gently blow on the fire.

Serves 2–4 as a middle course

2 pieces of marrow bone (each about 20cm long), cut in half lengthways
Hay Salt (page 283)
8 slices sourdough bread, toasted

Preheat the oven to 200°C.

Put the bones, cut side down, in a roasting tin. Roast until the marrow is soft and beginning to separate from the bones but remove before it starts to melt, about 15–20 minutes.

Serve the bone marrow warm with hay salt on the side and toasted sourdough bread.

Choux pastry with quince jam

74

This is a typical French pastry that we learned from one of our talented young co-workers, who bring their cultures into Ekstedt's kitchen to cook with our open fire. We serve the pastries with a sweet and tart quince jam. The choux makes ten buns and you will need four topped with craquelin for this recipe. Extra buns can be kept in an airtight container.

**Serves 2 as a dessert or
4 for a 'fika' (coffee snack)**

For the quince jam
400g quinces
juice of 2 lemons
30g sugar

For the buckwheat craquelin
20g brown sugar
20g buckwheat flour
20g unsalted butter, at room
    temperature

For the choux pastry
115g unsalted butter
120ml whole milk
¼ teaspoon sea salt
2 teaspoons sugar
65g buckwheat flour
65g rice flour
4 eggs

Start with the quince jam. Wash the quinces (no need to peel), then quarter and core them; keep the cores. Put the quarters into a large bowl, add the juice from 1 lemon and top up with water to cover; set aside. Put the cores into a medium saucepan with 1 litre water. Bring to the boil, then reduce the heat and leave to simmer for 1 hour.

Drain the quarters and cut into 1cm cubes. Put them into a large saucepan with the sugar and juice of the remaining lemon. Strain over the cooking liquid from the cores. Stir until the sugar dissolves, then bring to a simmer over a medium heat. Simmer for 45–60 minutes until the quince turns pink and the jam will set – test by putting a teaspoon of jam on a cold plate, waiting 30 seconds and then tilting the plate to make sure the jam says put. Pour the jam into a sterilised jar, cover with a lid and turn upside-down. Leave to cool before storing in the fridge for up to 3 months.

Mix together the brown sugar, buckwheat flour and butter for the craquelin. Spread out in a very thin layer (1mm) between two sheets of baking parchment on a tray. Freeze until firm.

To make the choux, put the butter, milk, salt and sugar in a saucepan with 120ml water and bring to a simmer over a medium heat, stirring until the butter has melted. Reduce the heat and add the flours all at once. Stir with a wooden spoon until the flour is completely incorporated, then keep stirring over the heat for 1–2 minutes.

Remove from the heat and transfer to the bowl of a stand mixer fitted with a paddle attachment. Cool down to room temperature, then, with the mixer running on low speed, add the eggs one at a time. When all the eggs have been added, the dough should look shiny, and be thick and smooth with a piping consistency. (The dough can be kept in the fridge for 5 days or frozen for 1 month. Return it to room temperature before using.)

Preheat the oven to 200°C.

Line baking trays with baking parchment and lightly brush the paper with water, which will create steam to help the pastry to puff up. Transfer the choux pastry to a piping bag fitted with a 5–8mm-wide tip. Pipe 3cm mounds of choux on the paper, about 5cm apart.

Using a 2cm round pastry cutter, cut out 4 rounds of craquelin (easiest if it is semi-frozen) and place on top of 4 of the choux buns.

Bake the buns for 12–15 minutes, then reduce the oven temperature to 175°C and continue to bake for 8–10 minutes until golden brown. Transfer the choux buns to a wire rack and leave to cool.

To serve, split open the 4 craquelin-topped choux buns horizontally and fill each with about ½ tablespoon of the quince jam.

Cloudberry doughnut

78

We usually serve a warm, just-baked pastry from our wood oven with a cup of coffee. It fills you with a wonderful feeling and reminds us of being in the mountains, setting up a fire and having a 'fika' (coffee snack). Our cast-iron-cooked doughnuts are served with the Nordic gold: cloudberries, which grow in the bogs of the Arctic tundra.

Makes 8: serves 4 as a dessert or 8 for a 'fika' (coffee snack)

100ml sparkling water
100g plain flour (preferably organic flour)
50g Clarified Butter (page 284), warmed to liquefy
8 tablespoons Vanilla Crème Pâtissière (page 286)
sea salt

For the cloudberry jam
120g cloudberries
1 tablespoon sugar

For the meadowsweet icing sugar
20 dried leaves of meadowsweet
2 tablespoons icing sugar

To make the jam, combine the cloudberries and sugar in a bowl and set aside at room temperature, stirring from time to time to help dissolve the sugar.

Meanwhile, put the sparkling water, flour and a pinch of salt in another bowl and whisk to a smooth batter. Leave to rest for 1 hour at room temperature.

Pound the dried meadowsweet leaves with the icing sugar in a mortar and pestle or blitz in a blender and set aside until ready to serve.

Preheat the oven to 220°C.

Heat a cast-iron doughnut pan (see page 289) in the oven. Remove the pan from the oven and place a teaspoon of clarified butter in each hole. Half fill each hole with doughnut batter. Put back into the oven and cook for 3–5 minutes until golden brown on the underside – check by carefully turning a doughnut with a spoon. Turn out the doughnuts on to a wire rack to cool slightly.

To serve, top each warm doughnut with a tablespoon each of crème pâtissière and cloudberry jam. Sift the meadowsweet icing sugar ever the top and serve immediately.

Almond financier with birch fudge

80

Birch wood is one of our most important 'ingredients' – we use it for the fires at the restaurant, as well as for seasoning. Infusing birch in cream, in combination with the flames from the fire in the wood oven, gives an almost vanilla-like flavour.

Serves 4 as a dessert

75g Browned Butter (page 285)
75g egg whites
75g icing sugar, sifted
30g almond flour
30g buckwheat flour
1 teaspoon baking powder
3 tablespoons melted butter, for brushing the moulds
6 almonds

For the birch fudge
500g double cream
100g sugar
10 sticks of birch wood (about 20cm long and 1–2cm diameter)

Preheat the oven to 225°C.

To make the fudge, combine the cream, sugar and birch sticks in a wide baking tin. Place in the oven and cook for about 30 minutes until reduced to a thick consistency. Leave to cool, then strain into a bowl.

Reduce the oven temperature to 140°C.

Heat the browned butter to liquefy it, then keep at around 50°C. Whisk the egg whites with an electric mixer until soft peaks form. Gradually add the sugar to the egg whites, a tablespoon at a time, whisking until the sugar dissolves. Fold in the almond flour, buckwheat flour and baking powder, then fold in the browned butter, a spoonful at the time.

Brush 4 small round moulds (about 100ml capacity) with the melted butter. Spoon the batter into the moulds, filling about halfway and top each with an almond. Bake for 10 minutes until a cake springs back when lightly pressed in the centre. Remove from the oven and cool slightly before carefully removing from the moulds. Place on a wire rack to cool completely.

Serve the financiers topped with a spoonful of birch fudge and grate the remaining almonds over the top.

Buckwheat sponge cake, milk ice cream & preserved cherries

Wood Oven
Autumn / Winter

82

The harvest of cherries in Sweden happens between July to August. By preserving the cherries for storage, we can enjoy a happy memory from sunny days during the colder autumn months.

Serves 4 as a dessert

For the preserved cherries
500g cherries
50ml port wine
5g sea salt

For the crispy buckwheat
2 tablespoons crushed
    buckwheat
1½ tablespoons rapeseed oil

For the milk ice cream
400ml milk
35g sugar
50g condensed milk
10g glucose

*For the buckwheat sponge
    cake*
30g unsalted butter, at room
    temperature, plus extra
    for greasing
125g caster sugar
4 eggs
125g buckwheat flour
1 teaspoon sea salt

First prepare the cherries. Cut them in half and remove the stones. Mix the cherries with the port and salt. Pack into a jar to fill and cover tightly. Invert the jar a couple of times to distribute the salt and port. Store in a cool place for 1–2 weeks, turning the jar over every day.

For the crispy buckwheat, soak the buckwheat in cold water for 12 hours. Drain and rinse in cold water a couple of times. Drain thoroughly in a sieve. Heat the oil in a frying pan and toast the buckwheat until golden brown, stirring occasionally. Drain on kitchen paper and cool before crushing roughly in a mortar with a pestle.

To make the ice cream, combine all the ingredients in a saucepan and bring to the boil over a medium-high heat, whisking to dissolve the sugar. Cool, then churn in an ice cream machine. Store in the freezer.

For the buckwheat sponge cake, preheat the oven to 180°C. Line the bottom of a 15cm round cake tin with baking parchment and grease the paper and the sides of the tin with butter.

Beat the butter with the sugar in a stand mixer until pale. Keep beating while adding the eggs, one at a time. Fold in the buckwheat flour and salt. Scoop the mixture into the tin; it will make a layer about 3cm deep. Bake for 25–30 minutes until the cake springs back when lightly pressed in the centre. Remove from the oven and cool before turning the cake out of the tin on to a wire rack.

To serve, cut the cake into quarters. Place a scoop or quenelle of ice cream on top of each portion of preserved cherries and top this with crispy buckwheat.

Smoked

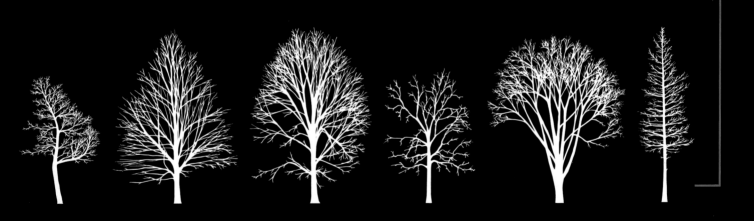

Smoked butter-poached scallop, sunflower emulsion & parsnip

Gently poaching fresh scallops in smoked butter gives them a delicate smoky aroma. We serve them with a seaweed sabayon, parsnip burnt in the flames of the fire and a nutty, creamy sunflower seed emulsion.

Serves 4 as a middle course

200g Smoked Butter (page 285)
2 teaspoons rapeseed oil
4 shelled scallops (without coral)
2 tablespoons Sunflower Seed Emulsion (page 281)
sea salt

For the flamed parsnip
1 large parsnip, about 20cm long
1 tablespoon Browned Butter (page 285)

For the seaweed sabayon
1 sheet nori seaweed
20ml lemon juice
140ml Vegetable Stock (page 278)
2 egg yolks (80g)

For the flamed parsnip, place it on top of the fire to cook in the flames for about 30 minutes until soft in the centre. Remove from the fire to cool, then peel and rub off the ash using your hands. Cut the parsnip into 3–5cm portions.

Make the sabayon just before serving. Blitz the seaweed with the lemon juice and vegetable stock in a small blender. Pour into a double boiler or a heatproof bowl set over a pan of simmering water and add the egg yolks. Whisk constantly over a medium heat to a foamy and creamy consistency.

Heat the smoked butter to 40°C in a pan just large enough to fit the scallops. In another pan, heat the rapeseed oil. Season the scallops with a pinch of salt and sear in the hot oil, then place in the warm smoked butter to poach for 1 minute (they should be covered with the butter). Meanwhile, sear the parsnip in the browned butter.

Top each scallop with sunflower seed emulsion. Serve with warm sabayon and flamed parsnip.

Hot-smoked herring, clams & heritage carrots

88

The most common fish in Sweden is probably herring, which is usually pickled. We eat it at pretty much every holiday – midsummer, Christmas and Easter. We even eat it fermented, or 'surströmming', with flatbread, soured cream, red onion and boiled almond potatoes. This might not be to everyone's taste, but it is traditional ... and schnapps and lager are part of the menu. In this recipe we smoke the herring straight on a burning log of birch.

In Sweden are there two varieties of herring: strömming and sill. Strömming live in the Baltic Sea with brackish water, while Sill are found in the south of the Baltic Sea and along the Swedish and Norwegian west coast. Sill are usually larger and fattier.

Serves 4 as a main course

4 herrings
sea salt

For the salt-baked carrots
300–500g coarse sea salt
3–6 carrots (preferably
  heritage carrots)

For the clams
20 fresh clams
90g butter
1 tablespoon Apple Cider
  Vinegar (page 280)

Preheat the oven to 200°C.

For the carrots, make a layer of sea salt about 3cm thick in a roasting tin. Place the carrots on top and bake for 20–30 minutes until they are tender. Remove from the oven and scrape off the skins using a tea towel. Cut each carrot in half lengthways and then into 3–5cm-long pieces.

Clean the herrings and cut off the fins and head. Butterfly each herring by removing the backbone but keeping the fillets attached to the skin in one piece. Season with a pinch of salt on each side. Set aside for 30 minutes.

Clean and rinse the clams in cold water. Drain. Heat a wide pan over a high heat. Add the clams, cover with a lid and steam for 3–4 minutes, stirring regularly, until all the clams are open. Remove from the heat and add the butter. Stir until the butter has melted, then add the vinegar. Strain the liquid into another pan and set aside. Reserve the clams.

Place each butterflied herring, skin side down, on a burning log to smoke for 3 minutes. Flip the herrings over and smoke for a further 1 minute. Meanwhile, heat the carrots and clams in the buttery clam jus. To serve, top the herrings with the clams, carrots and jus.

Swedish pancakes, smoked reindeer blood, puffed barley & apple purée

90

Reindeer in Sweden are semi-domesticated, herded by the Sami in the north. When we visited the Sami at the yearly autumn gathering we learned about using the blood; it has to be fresh and taken when still warm, then stirred until cold. Here we use reindeer blood for the traditional Swedish pancakes called 'plättar', which are small and thin, made in a cast-iron pan with seven round moulds. We serve them with crispy puffed barley, parsley and grilled apple purée.

Serves 12 as a snack or 4 as a middle course

For the puffed barley
2 tablespoons pearl barley
cooking oil, for deep-frying

For the pancakes
250ml reindeer blood
125ml ale
105g rye flour
35g butter, melted
½ tablespoon brown sugar
1 teaspoon sea salt
½ teaspoon ground cloves
½ teaspoon ground allspice
½ teaspoon ground dried
    marjoram
butter, for the pancake pan

For the crispy parsley
a bunch of curly parsley
100g Clarified Butter
    (page 284)
sea salt

To serve
200g Grilled Apple Purée
    (page 287)
lingonberries (page 288)

Preheat the oven to 60°C. Cook the barley in lightly salted water until tender. Drain and spread out in a roasting tin. Dry in the oven for about 2 hours. Heat the oil for deep-frying to 180°C and deep-fry the barley until golden brown. Drain on kitchen paper.

Put the reindeer blood in a wide saucepan and cold smoke for 10 minutes. Strain into a bowl. Add the remaining ingredients for the pancakes and whisk to a smooth batter. Cover with cling film and set aside for 30 minutes to swell.

Pick the parsley from the stems and fry in the clarified butter on a medium-high heat until crispy. Drain on kitchen paper and sprinkle with a pinch of salt.

Heat a cast-iron pancake pan until really hot. Using generous amounts of butter in each hole, fry 12 thin pancakes for about 30 seconds on each side. Top the pancakes with grilled apple purée, lingonberries, puffed barley and crispy parsley, and serve.

Hot-smoked crayfish, sole ceviche & apple vinegar

A crayfish party, or 'kräftskiva', is a popular summer celebration of eating and drinking in Sweden, traditionally held in late August at the time of the crayfish harvest. The succulent shellfish are boiled in salted water with dill flowers to be served cold and eaten with the fingers. Piled on large trays in the middle of the table, the crayfish are served with aged cheese and bread and butter.

At Ekstedt we cook the crayfish with flowering 'crowns' of dill, then let the fire pit give the shellfish a smokiness. In this recipe they are served with fresh sole from the west coast marinated in home-made apple cider vinegar.

Serves 4 as a middle course

For the fermented carrots
200g carrots of equal size
    and thickness
4g sea salt

For the hot-smoked crayfish
500ml lager
2 tablespoons brown sugar
60g sea salt
a bunch of flowering dill
    'crowns'
4 fresh crayfish

For the sole ceviche
150g skinless sole fillets
½ tablespoon Apple Cider
    Vinegar (page 280)
½ tablespoon cold-pressed
    rapeseed oil
1 teaspoon sea salt

To serve
12 carrot flowers and leaves,
    to garnish

For the fermented carrots, peel the carrots and cut lengthways into equal pieces about 1.5cm in diameter. Combine the carrots with the salt in a plastic bag and press out as much air as possible. Seal the bag and leave at room temperature for 1 week, then for 2 more weeks in the refrigerator. For serving, remove 50g of the carrots and cut across into thin discs. (Decant the remaining carrots, with liquid, into a covered jar; they will keep in the fridge for 1 week.)

Prepare the crayfish the day before serving. Put the beer, sugar, salt and half of the dill in a pan with 1 litre water. Bring to the boil, then simmer for 5 minutes. Add the crayfish and remaining dill. Increase the heat and bring back to the boil. Remove the pan from the heat and leave the crayfish to cool down in the liquid until the next day.

Cut the sole fillets into 2 x 2cm pieces and combine with the vinegar, oil and salt. Set aside for 5 minutes.

Cut 2 of the crayfish in half lengthways and hot smoke for 2–3 minutes. Peel the other 2 crayfish tails and slice into 1.5cm pieces. Top the sole ceviche with pieces of crayfish, fermented carrot slices, and carrot flowers and leaves. Remove the smoked crayfish tails from the shells and add to the dish.

Pine-smoked mussels

96

The special way of cooking mussels in burning pine needles is called 'eclade' in France. It originated with mussel fishermen in Bordeaux. The mussels are arranged on a wood plank and buried under a thick layer of dried pine needles, which is set on fire. The heat from the flames opens the mussels. We've adapted this, to steam open the mussels and then smoke them at the table with dried pine needles, to serve with a mayonnaise-like mussel emulsion.

Serves 2–4 as a snack

1kg mussels
a bunch of dried pine needles

For the mussel emulsion
10 mussels
1 tablespoon chopped
    shallots
½ garlic clove, chopped
a sprig of thyme
50ml dry white wine
50ml Smoked Oil (page 283)

*For the parsley and
    garlic paste*
100ml olive oil
2 garlic cloves, peeled
10g parsley leaves
1 teaspoon sea salt

Start with the mussel emulsion. Clean and rinse the mussels in cold water; drain. Heat a wide pan over a high heat. Add the mussels, shallots, garlic, thyme and wine. Cover with a lid and steam for 3–4 minutes until the mussels are open, stirring every minute.

Remove from the heat and pick the mussels out of their shells. Strain the liquid into a wide pan and reduce by half over a medium-high heat. Leave to cool, then add the shelled mussels. Cold smoke for 30 minutes. Tip into a blender and blitz to a smooth consistency. Keep the machine running and gradually add the smoked oil, to emulsify to a mayonnaise-like consistency.

Put all the ingredients for the parsley and garlic paste into a small blender and blitz until smooth. (This will make more paste than you need for this recipe. The remainder can be kept in the fridge for a day. Or pass it through a sieve and use it as a herb oil – keep this in the fridge for up to 3 days.)

Clean and rinse the kilo of mussels in cold water; drain. Heat a wide pan over a high heat. Add the mussels, cover with a lid and steam for 3–4 minutes until the mussels are open, stirring every minute. Remove from the heat and add 1 tablespoon of the parsley and garlic paste. Stir well.

Spread out the pine needles in a wide cast-iron pan. Place the cooked mussels on the needles, shell side down. Set the needles alight, then cover with a lid or foil to kill the fire and start it smoking. Smoke for 2 minutes. Remove the lid and serve the mussels with the mussel emulsion.

Ember

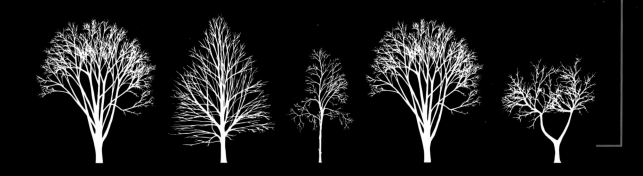

Onion confit purée & Brussels sprouts

Ember
Autumn / Winter

Sweden is a country with four more or less equally long seasons of three months each, so fresh vegetables are something we enjoy from May through to October. The rest of the year we use vegetables suitable for long keeping, such as potatoes, cabbage, salsify, parsnips, onions, celeriac and beetroot, all of which are kept in underground storehouses. One vegetable that is unique in being harvested during the winter is the Brussels sprout. We serve it roasted as a snack with ember-cooked onion confit.

Serves 2–4 as a snack

16 Brussels sprouts
1 tablespoon Clarified Butter
    (page 284)

For the onion confit
2 large onions (unpeeled)
sea salt

Place the onions in the embers of the fire and cook for about 30 minutes until tender, turning them every 5 minutes. Remove from the embers and cool down. Peel the onions (save the burnt skin) and place in a roasting tin. Cold smoke for 30 minutes. Blitz the smoked onion in a blender to a smooth, creamy consistency and season with salt.

Trim off any dirty outer leaves from the Brussels sprouts, then cut off 1 or 2 leaves from each sprout. Blanch the leaves in salted boiling water for 3 seconds. Drain and cool down in iced water.

Cut the Brussels sprouts in half and sear in the clarified butter until golden brown. Serve with the blanched sprout leaves and onion confit, and sprinkle some burnt onion skin on top.

Roast pork, pickled kohlrabi, bread-baked chanterelle & kale cocotte

104

Grill-searing pork sirloin and then slowly cooking it is a great technique to keep it nice and tender. We serve it in the autumn with sweet and sour pickled kohlrabi and freshly harvested kohlrabi cooked in the flames of the open fire.

Serves 4 as a main course

2 pieces of boneless pork
    sirloin, about 300g each
sea salt

For the pork jus
2.5kg pork ribs
1 onion, cut in half
2 carrots, cut in half
2 celery sticks
5 sprigs of thyme

For the pickled kohlrabi
50ml ättika (page 288)
100g sugar
1–2 kohlrabi (you want 150g
    peeled weight)

For the burnt kohlrabi
1 kohlrabi, weighing about
    150g

*For the chanterelle and kale
    cocottes*
1 tablespoon lard
180g plain flour
200g chanterelles
15g butter
100g kale
1 egg yolk mixed with
    1 tablespoon water

Preheat the oven to 80°C.

Grill the pork ribs over the embers until golden brown. Also grill the onion and carrots on all sides.

Put the ribs, onion, carrots, celery and thyme in a deep roasting tin and cover with water. Cover with a lid or foil and cook in the oven for 10 hours. Strain and reduce to a glaze consistency. Season with salt.

To pickle the kohlrabi, combine the ättika, sugar, 1 teaspoon salt and 150ml water in a saucepan and bring to the boil, whisking to dissolve the sugar and salt. Remove from the heat and leave to cool. Meanwhile, peel the kohlrabi, then shave on a mandolin into 1mm slices. Place in a bowl, cover with the pickling liquid and leave at room temperature for 2 hours, then keep in the fridge.

For the burnt kohlrabi, place the whole kohlrabi on a grill rack in the fire, about 20cm above the burning log. Cook for about 30 minutes, turning every 5 minutes, until tender and cooked all the way through; test with a skewer. The skin will burn and blacken. Remove from the heat and cool to room temperature before peeling off the burnt skin – this is easiest using your hands. Cut into quarters. Before serving, heat up the kohlrabi in the oven.

For the cocottes, bring 100ml water with 1 teaspoon salt to the boil in a saucepan over a high heat. Add the lard and stir until it melts. Cool down to room temperature. Add the flour and mix in, then knead to a quite stiff, dry dough. Add more flour if needed. Set aside to rest for 1 hour.

Heat the oven to 175°C.

Trim the skin from the pork, leaving about 1cm of fat. Score the fat into 2–3cm squares. Season with salt. Place the pork in a cold pan, fat side down. Set over a medium-high heat and cook until the fat is golden brown and caramelised. Remove the pork from the pan and grill quickly over medium-high embers on the remaining sides – not too long, just to make grill marks. Place somewhere close to the embers, or in the oven at 80–120°C, and cook slowly to an internal temperature of 60°C. Remove from the heat and leave to rest while you finish the cocottes.

Roll out the dough thinly and cut out 4 circles that are 2cm larger in diameter than the cocottes you will be using for the chanterelles and kale. Sauté the chanterelles in the butter. Season with salt and drain on kitchen paper. Rip the kale off the stems into pieces about 3 x 3cm.

Divide the kale and chanterelles among 4 cast-iron cocottes. Pour ½ tablespoon pork jus into each one. Cover each with a dough lid and attach this to the rim. Brush with the egg yolk wash to glaze. Bake for 6–8 minutes until golden brown.

Reheat 200ml of the pork jus, then season with about 1 tablespoon of the kohlrabi pickling liquid, or to taste. (If you have any jus left over, it keeps well in the freezer.)

Sear the pork quickly on all sides, to heat up the surface, then cut each loin in half and serve with the pickled kohlrabi, warm burnt kohlrabi and pork jus, with the bread-baked cocottes on the side.

Grilled lobster, broth, pickled mushrooms & porcini

A warm and rich consommé with lobsters and porcini – two of the most beautiful foods of the autumn season.

Serves 2–4 as a middle course

2 live lobsters
2 tablespoons Clarified
    Butter (page 284
a bunch of chickweed
sea salt

For the lobster broth
3 shallots, thinly sliced
2 garlic cloves, thinly sliced
15g butter
500ml Chicken Stock (page
    279)
1 bay leaf
4 sprigs of thyme

For the pickled mushrooms
1 garlic clove, cut into
    quarters
100ml extra virgin olive oil
50ml Apple Cider Vinegar
    (page 280)
50ml white wine
100g fresh porcini, cut into
    2cm dice
3 black peppercorns
1 bay leaf

For the butter-sautéed porcini
1 large fresh porcini
15g butter

Put 150g sea salt into a large pan with 5 litres water and bring to the boil. Add the lobsters and cover with a lid. Cook for 3 minutes. Lift out the lobsters and cool in iced water.

Pull away the claws and tail from each lobster. Remove the meat from the claws and tail in whole pieces and set aside. Keep all the shells and the lobster heads. Open the bodies and remove the grey feathery gills; discard. Roughly crush all the lobster shells.

Sauté the shallots and garlic in the butter in a wide pan. Add the crushed lobster shells and sauté for 2–3 minutes. Add the chicken stock, bay leaf and thyme and bring to the boil, then simmer for 20 minutes. Remove from the heat and sit aside for 1 hour. Strain into a clean pan and season with salt. Set aside, ready to reheat for serving.

To pickle the mushrooms, sauté the garlic in 1 tablespoon of the olive oil without colouring it. Add the vinegar and white wine and bring to the boil. Simmer until reduced by half. Add the diced porcini, peppercorns and bay leaf and simmer for a further 20 minutes. Remove from the heat, add the rest of the olive oil and leave the mushrooms to cool in the liquid.

Clean the large porcini and cut into 3 x 3cm pieces. Sauté in the butter until golden brown.

Brush the lobster claws with 1 tablespoon of the clarified butter, then hot smoke for 4–6 minutes until cooked all the way through.

Grill the lobster tails over embers at a high heat for 2–3 minutes on each side. Finish by brushing the lobster tails with the remaining clarified butter and placing back over the embers for 30 seconds.

Drain the pickled porcini and divide among 2–4 bowls. Top with the butter-sautéed porcini, grilled lobster tails and hot-smoked lobster claws, then add a couple of stems of chickweed and the hot lobster broth.

Grilled cod, bottarga & crushed potatoes

We use cod's roe to make a Nordic version of the Italian bottarga. The roe is salted, cured, smoked and slowly dried above the fire pit in the kitchen, which gives it a delicate smoky aroma. Here the bottarga is served with cod fillet, grilled gently over a medium-high heat, then rested on the side of the fire to keep it moist.

Serves 4 as a main course

4 pieces of skinless cod fillet, each about 140g
4 tablespoons Crispy Potato (page 282)
sea salt

For the bottarga
1 cod's roe, about 400g

For the crushed potatoes
500g potatoes (a tasty variety), unpeeled
3 tablespoons Smoked Butter (page 285)

For the fish foam
200ml fish stock
45g butter
2 teaspoons ättika (page 288)
2 tablespoons herb oil (page 283)

Start with the bottarga. Clean the cod's roe to remove all blood and clots. Cold smoke the roe for 30 minutes. Meanwhile, put 1 litre water in a pan, add 1½ teaspoons salt and bring to the boil, whisking to dissolve the salt. Pour this brine into a bowl and leave to cool. Add the cod's roe (it should be completely submerged in the brine) and leave in the fridge for 24 hours.

Lift out the roe and drain on kitchen paper. Place on a tray and store somewhere dry and cold for 5–10 days. When ready the roe will be quite firm to the touch and able to be sliced.

For the crushed potatoes, cook the potatoes in boiling, lightly salted water. Drain and steam off excess moisture. Crush the potatoes roughly with the smoked butter in a large mortar with a pestle (or in a bowl using the end of a rolling pin). Season with salt and keep warm.

Season the cod and grill over embers at a medium-high heat. When done the internal temperature will be 48°C. Allow to rest for 3 minutes.

Meanwhile, heat up the fish stock. Add the butter and ättika, then blitz to a foam with a stick blender. Add the herb oil to the foam and fold in carefully so you keep foamy consistency.

Serve the cod with slices of bottarga, the fish foam and the crushed potatoes topped with the crispy potatoes.

High-hanged roast beef ribeye & turnip

112

Slow-cooking a ribeye joint over the fire is simple and straightforward. Let it take its time and then make sure you rest the meat before serving. We cook it hanging about 60cm above the flames, depending on the size of the fire. A useful trick is to keep it a bit to the side of the flames so the fat from the meat does not drip down directly into the fire.

Serves 4 as a main course

about 500g coarse sea salt
500g turnips
95g unsalted butter
1 x 1kg well-aged dairy beef/
    Basque beef (page 288),
    bone-in ribeye joint
3 tablespoons Beef
    Demiglace (page 280)
sea salt

Preheat the oven to 175°C.

Spread a bed of coarse sea salt in a roasting tin and place the turnips on top. Bake for 30–45 minutes until soft. Cool, then peel the turnips, saving the skin. Cut 4 pieces of turnip about 3 x 3cm and set aside.

Blitz the remaining peeled turnips in a blender with 80g of the butter to a smooth, shiny consistency. Season with salt. Set aside, ready to reheat for serving.

Clean and scrape 12 pieces of the saved turnip skin. Dry in the oven at 60°C for about 2 hours.

Allow the beef to warm up to room temperature. Season both sides generously with sea salt. Place bone-side down on a cast-iron grill rack on top of the embers at around 80°C. Cook for about 1 hour, then turn the meat fat-side down and keep cooking until it reaches an internal temperature of 48°C. Cooking time will be about 1½ hours in total. Remove from the heat and allow to rest for 15 minutes.

Take the beef from the bone and cut into 4 steaks. Pan-fry the pieces of turnip in the remaining butter until golden brown. Add 1 tablespoon beef demiglace to glaze the turnip. Serve the beef with the warm turnip purée, glazed turnip, dried turnip skin and remaining beef demiglace.

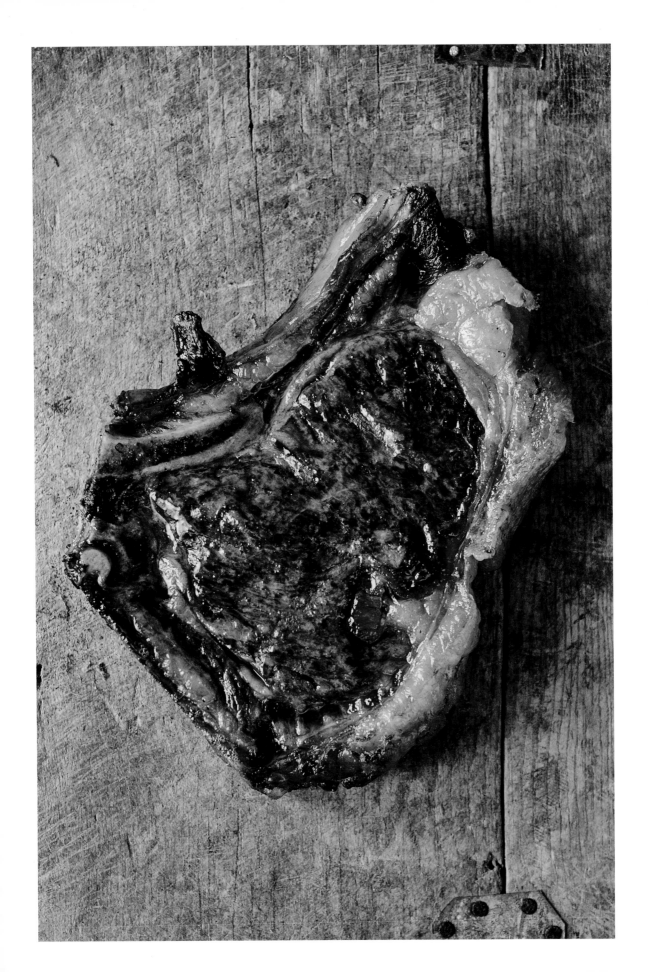

Almond cake, grilled apple ice cream & tea caramel

Cooking apples over the embers adds a sweet and caramelised flavour to this ice cream.

Serves 4 as a dessert

For the almond cakes
120g almond paste
60g unsalted butter, at room
    temperature, plus extra
    for greasing
1 egg

For the apple ice cream
130g sugar
200g Grilled Apple Purée
    (page 287)
125g cream cheese
125g soured cream

For the tea-leaf caramel
90g sugar
1 tablespoon black tea leaves
4 sweet cecily leaves

For the caramelised apple
1 large eating apple
1 tablespoon Clarified Butter
    (page 284)
1 teaspoon icing sugar

Preheat the oven to 180°C. Line the bottom of 4 small round tins (about 8cm in diameter) with baking parchment, then grease the paper and the side of the tins with butter.

Using an electric mixer, beat the almond paste with the butter to a smooth consistency. Keep beating as you add the egg. Scoop the mixture into the tins, to make a layer about 3cm deep. Bake for 15–20 minutes until a skewer inserted into the centre of a cake comes out clean. Remove from the oven and leave to cool, then turn out of the tins and place the cakes on a wire rack. Leave the oven on.

To make the ice cream, put the sugar in a saucepan with 1 tablespoon water and bring to the boil over a high heat. Lower the heat and simmer to 150°C to caramelise. Add the apple purée and keep simmering to dissolve the caramelised sugar. Allow to cool before mixing with the cream cheese and soured cream. Churn in an ice cream machine, then store in the freezer.

For the tea-leaf caramel, combine the sugar with 200ml water in a saucepan and bring to the boil, stirring to dissolve the sugar. Remove from the heat. Add the tea, cover with a lid and leave to infuse for 10 minutes. Strain into a clean saucepan and bring to the boil over a high heat. Lower the heat and simmer to 150°C to caramelise. Pour on to a tray in a thin layer and leave to cool and set.

Cut thin slices from the 4 sides of the apple. Make 4 stacks of slices, 8–10 in each stack, and trim the stacks into pieces about 4cm long and 2cm wide. Place skin side up in a tin. Heat the clarified butter to liquefy it, then brush over the apple skin. Sprinkle with the icing sugar. Cook in the 180°C oven to caramelise.

Place a scoop or quenelle of ice cream on each almond cake. Crack a few small pieces of tea caramel on top of the ice cream, then top with sweet cecily. Serve the warm caramelised apple on the side.

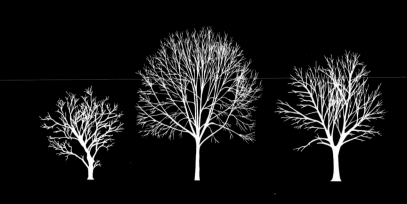

Hay-flamed

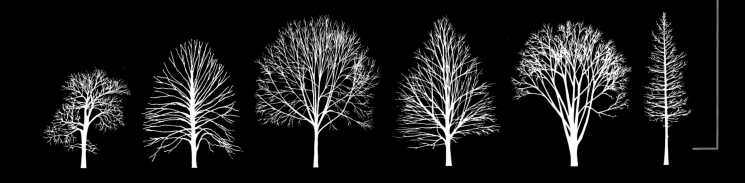

Venison tataki & pickled unripe blackcurrants

Hay-flamed

Autumn / Winter

Blackcurrants, as well as red or white currants, are common berries in Swedish home gardens, used to make jam and summer drinks, among other things. When they are green, we treat them almost like capers, preserving them with Swedish vinegar to give acidity and saltiness to many dishes. Here the capers are served to complement lightly-seared venison. Make sure your pan is really hot for searing the meat – this is best achieved using a cast-iron pan, which will maintain the heat.

Serves 4 as a main course

1 x 240g venison fillet
1 tablespoon rapeseed oil
a handful of hay
2 teaspoons sliced spring
    onion, to garnish
sea salt and freshly ground
    black pepper

*For the pickled unripe
    blackcurrants*
200g unripe/green
    blackcurrants
100ml ättika (page 288)
20g sugar

*For the beetroot-marinated
    red onion*
½ red onion, thinly sliced
2 tablespoons red beetroot
    juice
2 tablespoons white wine
    vinegar

Pack the ingredients for the pickled blackcurrants into a sterilised jar with 2 teaspoons salt. Cover with a lid. Leave at room temperature for 1 week, turning the jar over once a day, then store cold for 1 week before using. (Any pickled blackcurrants not used for this recipe can be kept in the fridge for 6 months.)

For the beetroot-marinated red onion, combine the onion with the beetroot juice, vinegar and ½ teaspoon salt in a jar or bowl. Cover and store cold for 5 days before using. (The marinated onion can be kept in the fridge for up to 1 week.)

Season the venison with salt and pepper and brush with the oil. Sear in a smoking-hot cast-iron pan for 2–3 seconds on each side. Transfer to the grill rack over the wood fire and place the handful of hay underneath. Set the hay alight and burn for about 20 seconds. Finish by coating the meat with some of the hay ash.

Cut the venison into 3mm slices. Spread out the slices and scatter 2 tablespoons each of the pickled blackcurrants and beetroot-marinated red onion over them along with the sliced spring onion.

Whole baked swede, winter truffle & spinach

122   The sweetness of slow-cooked swede is enhanced by the aroma from the truffle.

Serves 4 as a middle course

2 swedes
a handful of hay
20g black winter truffle,
   thinly shaved
50g spinach

For the green oil
100ml rapeseed oil
50g spinach
50g green top of leek
50g chervil

Burn the swedes over the open fire, turning, until the skin is silver all over and the swedes are cooked through (test with a skewer). Leave to rest for 30 minutes, then scrape off the burnt skin and cut each swede into 2 nice cylinder shapes about 1cm thick. Reserve in a cast-iron pan ready for hay flaming.

For the green oil, heat the oil to 60°C. Put all the greens in a blender with the oil and blitz until smooth. Pass through a muslin-lined sieve. (Any oil not used for this recipe can be kept in the fridge for 2 days.)

Cover the swede with hay. Set alight and let it burn to ashes. Brush off the ash, then serve the swede with the truffle shavings, fresh spinach and 2 tablespoons green oil.

Scallops, hay & coral

124

This recipe uses diver-caught wild scallops, fresh from the coast of Norway.
It's such a simple recipe, but when you have such great produce you don't need
to do much.

Serves 4 as a middle course

4 fresh scallops in their shells
1 teaspoon sea salt
1 teaspoon rapeseed oil
2 tablespoons white wine
   vinegar
100g Smoked Butter (page
   285)
a handful of hay

Carefully open each scallop shell and remove the white muscle (the
scallop) and the coral. Clean them and discard the guts. Set the 4 corals
aside for the paste. Season the scallops with the sea salt, then sear one side
in the oil in a smoking-hot cast-iron pan. Transfer the scallops to a clean
pan, placing them seared side up.

For the coral paste, blitz the corals with the vinegar in a small blender or
food processor. Pass the purée through a fine chinois into a bowl. Warm
the smoked butter to 45°C, then whisk it (or blitz with a stick blender)
drop by drop into the coral purée to emulsify.

Cover the scallops with hay. Set it alight and let it burn to ashes. Brush
the ash off the scallops and serve with the coral paste.

Hay-flamed char, samphire sabayon & kohlrabi

128

Here hot-smoked char seasoned with flamed hay is paired with kohlrabi cooked in the flames and served with a sabayon seasoned with saltiness from fresh samphire.

Serves 4 as a middle course

1 Arctic char, about 700g,
  cleaned
1 teaspoon sea salt
a handful of hay
12 fresh samphire spears

For the burnt kohlrabi
1 kohlrabi, about 300g

For the samphire sabayon
200g fresh samphire
1 tablespoon soy sauce
1 tablespoon white wine
  vinegar
2 egg yolks

Fillet the char and remove the pinbones. Season the fillets with the salt, then hot smoke to an internal temperature of 35°C. Peel off the skin (if you like, keep the skin for Flambadou Arctic Char and Crispy Skin, page 158). Cut the fish into 4 x 50g portions. (The remaining fish can be frozen and used in another recipe, such as a fish soup or ceviche, or to make Flambadou Arctic Char and Crispy Skin.) Place the pieces of fish in a roasting tin, ready for hay flaming.

For the burnt kohlrabi, place the whole kohlrabi on a grill rack in the fire, about 20cm above the burning log. Cook for about 30 minutes, turning every 5 minutes, until tender and cooked all the way through; test with a skewer. The skin will burn and blacken. Remove from the heat and cool to room temperature before peeling off the burnt skin – this is easiest using your hands. Cut into 4 pieces.

To make the samphire sabayon, pass the samphire through a juicer: you want 100ml of juice. Mix the juice with the soy sauce and vinegar, then add the egg yolks and strain through a fine chinois into a saucepan (or the top of a double boiler or a heatproof bowl). Reserve.

To serve, cover the char with hay and set it alight. Burn to ashes. Heat up the burnt kohlrabi in the oven. Meanwhile, place the pan of sabayon over a medium-high heat (or set the top of the double boiler or bowl over a pan of simmering water) and beat hard with a whisk to a foamy consistency. Serve the fish with the kohlrabi garnished with samphire spears, and the sabayon alongside.

Butternut squash, fermented salsify & vegetable foam

130

Fresh from the fire, this dish combines delicate grilled salad with tart and crispy fermented salsify and smokiness from the burnt hay and fresh lovage.

Serves 4 as a middle course

1 butternut squash
15g butter
a handful of hay
a bunch of lovage

For the fermented salsify
4 salsify
sea salt

For the hay-flamed salsify
1 salsify, about 25cm long
a handful of hay

For the vegetable foam
200ml Vegetable Stock (page 278)
80g cold unsalted butter

For the grilled sweetcorn
1 corn on the cob, leaves and 'silk' removed

For the grilled salad
2 leaves of frisée
2 green salad leaves
1 teaspoon Smoked Butter (page 285)

First prepare the fermented salsify. Peel the salsify, then weigh it – you want to add 2 per cent of the weight in sea salt. Mix the salsify with the salt and keep in a closed container for 10 days at room temperature.

Cut off the bulbous part of the squash. Cut 4 cylindrical slices about 1cm thick from the remaining squash. Keep the rest of the squash, with the bulbous part, for another dish. Gently pan-fry the squash slices in the butter until they are soft in texture. Peel off the skin and cut each slice in half to obtain half-moon shapes. Lay the pieces in a pan, ready for hay flaming.

For the hay-flamed salsify, burn the salsify over the open fire until the skin turns silver. Allow to cool for 30 minutes, then peel off the burnt skin. Cut into 4 portions, then reserve in a pan ready for hay flaming.

Heat up the vegetable stock for the foam – it needs to be around 70°C in order to foam correctly with the action of a stick blender.

For the grilled sweetcorn, grill it whole on the grill rack for 4–6 minutes on each side. Cut off portions of kernels from the cob.

For the grilled salad, gently grill the leaves in a metal chinois in contact with the fire's embers for 3 seconds, then drizzle with the smoked butter.

To finish, cover the butternut squash and salsify with hay and set it alight. Let it burn out, then brush off the ash.

Add the butter and a spoon or two of juice from the fermented salsify, to taste, to the warm vegetable stock and blitz to a foam with a stick blender. Assemble the elements of the dish (the hay-flamed butternut squash and salsify, 4 pieces of fermented salsify and the grilled salad and sweetcorn) and serve with the vegetable foam and a garnish of lovage.

Salmon, hay salt & wild garlic capers

Hay-flamed

Autumn / Winter

134

Wild garlic, also called ramsons, grows wild in the south of Sweden, up to a latitude just north of Stockholm. The buds are picked after flowering in early summer to be preserved with salt and vinegar. These capers make a great combo with fat salmon smoked with hay.

Serves 4 as a middle course

1 x 300g piece of fresh wild
   salmon loin (skinless fillet)
a handful of hay
100g Wild Garlic Capers
   (page 281)
½ tablespoon Hay Salt
   (page 283)
fine salt

Season the salmon generously with fine salt, then set aside at room temperature for 10 minutes. Rinse in ice-cold water to remove any impurities. This salting will make the flesh nice and firm.

Drop the salmon on a grill rack and set the hay alight beneath it. Gently roll the salmon so it is evenly seared by the flames, allowing about 15–20 seconds on each side. Chill in the fridge for about 30 minutes before cutting into 4 portions (it's easier to cut when cold).

Serve the salmon with the wild garlic capers and hay salt.

Open Fire

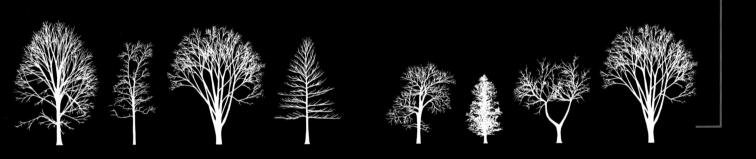

Beef tartare, lingonberry, sourdough croutons & ash mayo

138

Hand-cut dry-aged sirloin tartare is served raw with crispy croutons and ash-infused mayonnaise. The mayonnaise in combination with the raw beef adds a deeper flavour of the open-fire to the dish.

Serves 4 as a middle course

200g dry-aged beef sirloin
2 tablespoons lingonberries
   (page 288)
sea salt

For the ash mayonnaise
3 leek leaves, green part only,
   about 20cm long
1 egg yolk
½ tablespoon mustard
1 teaspoon Apple Cider
   Vinegar (page 280)
150ml rapeseed oil

For the sourdough croutons
1 slice sourdough bread
2 tablespoons Clarified
   Butter (page 284)

Preheat the oven to 225°C.

For the mayonnaise, clean the leek leaves in cold water. Spread out in a roasting tin and place in the oven. Bake until totally burnt. Cool, then blitz in a small food processor to a powder.

Whisk together the egg yolk, mustard, vinegar and a pinch of salt. Keep whisking while you add the oil drop by drop until emulsified. Season with 1 tablespoon burnt leek powder, or to taste.

To make the croutons, trim off the crusts and cut the bread into 5mm dice. Cook in the clarified butter until golden brown. Drain on a rack. Chop finely.

To serve, cut the sirloin into 10mm dice. Serve topped with the ash mayonnaise, lingonberries and croutons.

Pork spare ribs, bbq plum glaze & salt-baked young carrots

140

In this recipe we grill the plums quite hard, to get the skin a bit burnt. The bitterness of the charred skin balances the natural sweetness of the plum flesh, making a deliciously smoky, sweet and sour bbq sauce or glaze.

Serves 4 as a middle course

a slab of 8 meaty pork
    spare ribs
8 young carrots
rapeseed flowers, to garnish
sea salt

For the bbq plum glaze
6 plums (about 300g in total)
5–6 black peppercorns
1 tablespoon Apple Cider
    Vinegar (page 280)

Dissolve 1 tablespoon salt in 1 litre water, whisking to dissolve the salt. Add the ribs, making sure they are covered in liquid. Leave to brine in the fridge for 10 hours.

Drain the ribs. Roast gently over the flames at about 120°C for 2–3 hours. Start bone side down and turn over after the first hour, then back to bone side after 30 minutes. The ribs are ready when cooked firm in the centre: check with a skewer or paring knife. Set aside to rest for 30 minutes.

Preheat the oven to 130–150°C.

Grill the whole plums on 4 sides to mark with charred stripes. Remove from the heat and place in a baking tray. Add the peppercorns and cover with foil. Bake in the oven for 2 hours until the plums are completely soft and collapsed. Remove the stones from the plums. Blitz in a blender to a smooth paste and season with the vinegar.

Spread out a 2cm-thick layer of salt on a baking tray. Place the carrots on top and bake in the oven at 150°C for about 30 minutes until tender but still firm in the centre. Remove from the oven and cool for 5 minutes. Cut each carrot in half lengthways.

Bone the ribs, 2 pieces per portion. Brush with the plum sauce and place over medium-high embers to glaze for 5 minutes, brushing with the plum sauce every minute or so. Serve with the salt-baked carrots and garnish with rapeseed flowers.

Sweetbreads, kale, Japanese mushrooms & bone marrow glaze

142

During the winter we like to use organic farmed mushrooms to add freshness to the stored root vegetables and fermentations from the autumn harvest.

Serves 4 as a middle course

4 pieces of veal sweetbreads, blanched, peeled and trimmed, about 40g each (weight after preparation)
1 tablespoon spelt flour
1 tablespoon rapeseed oil
30g butter

For the seared mushrooms
100g mixed Japanese mushrooms (enoki, shimeji, shiitake)
1 tablespoon Browned Butter (page 285)

For the grilled kale
100g kale leaves
2 tablespoons Smoked Butter (page 285)

For the bone marrow glaze
20g fresh bone marrow
100g Beef Demiglace (page 280)

For the seared mushrooms, pan-fry the mushrooms quickly in the browned butter and set aside.

For the grilled kale, brush the kale with the smoked butter, then grill over the fire.

For the bone marrow glaze, add the marrow to the cold demiglace in a pan and bring up to serving temperature, melting the marrow and emulsifying the demiglace.

Coat the sweetbreads with the spelt flour, then fry in the oil in a smoking-hot cast-iron pan for 2–3 minutes, turning to brown all over. At the end, add the butter and, as it melts, generously bathe the sweetbreads.

Serve the sweetbreads with the pan-fried mushrooms, grilled kale and bone marrow glaze.

Baba au rhum, preserved plums & sorbet

144

Here is our variation of the classic French dessert named after a character in *One Thousand and One Nights* (or *Arabian Nights*). The original recipe is said to have used brandy but we use rum and serve the babas with slightly salty fermented plums and grilled plum ice cream.

Serves 4 as a dessert

150g plain flour
2g fine salt
55g unsalted butter, at room
    temperature
6g fresh yeast
1 tablespoon honey
3 eggs

For the preserved plums
500g plums
40g sea salt

For the syrup
50g sugar
1–2 tablespoons rum

For the plum sorbet
600g plums
60g sugar
3 tablespoons plum brandy

For the preserved plums, combine the plums and salt and pack into a sterilised jar. Cover tightly. Store in a dark place, at room temperature (18–20°C), for 1 month before using. (You can reduce the quantities, but any leftover preserved plums will keep well in the fridge for 1 month.)

For the babas au rhum, put the flour, salt, butter, yeast and honey in a stand mixer fitted with a whisk. Mix on low speed for 3 minutes to obtain a crumbly texture. Keep mixing while adding the eggs, one at a time, then mix for a further 3 minutes on medium speed. Scrape the side of the bowl and mix at high speed for 7 minutes to obtain an elastic dough.

Transfer the dough into 4 baba moulds, half filling each of them. Leave to rise at room temperature for about 1 hour until the dough has doubled in size and risen almost to the top of the mould.

Preheat the oven to 190°C.

Bake the babas for about 15 minutes until they spring back when lightly pressed with a fingertip. Turn out gently on to a wire rack and leave to cool.

To make the syrup, put the sugar and 500ml water in a saucepan and bring to the boil. Remove from the heat and stir in the rum. Set aside to cool.

For the plum sorbet, cut the plums in half and remove the stones. Place the plums skin side down on the grill rack over the fire and grill over a medium-high heat for 6–8 minutes until semi-soft and marked with grill lines. Transfer to a saucepan and cook the plums with the sugar and plum brandy until soft. Pass through a chinois and cool, then freeze in a Pacojet.

Soak the babas in the rum syrup for 5 minutes. Brush them with syrup just before serving to make them shiny. Cut the some preserved plums into wedges. Serve the babas with the preserved plums and plum sorbet.

Flambadou

Flambadou oysters, smoked apple & beurre blanc

A beautiful combination of aromas and textures from the fatty flambadou-cooked oysters, smoked crisp apple pearl and smooth butter sauce. On the menu for many years, this is a signature dish of the restaurant.

Serves 2–4 as a snack

4 oysters
1 x 15g piece of beef fat or
   tallow from dry-aged beef
   (page 288)
4 nasturtium leaves, to
   garnish

For the smoked apple
1 tart, firm eating apple
juice of ½ lemon

For the beurre blanc
200g cold unsalted butter, cut
   into 2cm dice
1 teaspoon ättika (page 288)
   or white wine vinegar
sea salt

Open the oysters carefully, keeping the jus. Rinse the oysters to be sure there are no shell fragments, then place in a small bowl with the jus and refrigerate for 10 minutes. Reserve the bottom shells for serving.

Peel the apple and scoop out 4 pearls of flesh about 1.5cm in diameter. Place in a bowl containing 200ml water and the lemon juice and set aside for 10–20 minutes. Drain, then cold smoke the apple pearls for 10 minutes.

To make the beurre blanc, scoop out 2 tablespoons jus from the oysters and strain it through a fine sieve into a small frying pan. Place the frying pan over a low heat. Add the butter, a cube at a time, whisking constantly – add another cube only when the previous cube has been completely incorporated. (It's important to use chilled butter; if it is warm it may melt too quickly, making it harder to incorporate into the liquid and causing the mixture to split.)

Once all the butter is incorporated, which will take 3–4 minutes, remove from the heat and add the ättika. Season with salt, depending on the saltiness of the oyster jus. Keep warm in a bain marie, covered with a lid or cling film.

Place the oysters on an untreated wood plank. Sear each oyster for 4–6 seconds with burning beef fat from the flambadou.

Transfer the oysters to their bottom shells. Spoon the beurre blanc on to the oysters and top each with a smoked apple pearl and a nasturtium leaf. Serve immediately.

Brussels sprouts, smoked parsley root & plum sauce

150

Parsley root is one of the beautiful root vegetables we are lucky to find locally.
In this dish the parsley root is smoked and dried to grate as an aromatic powder
on top of fresh Brussels sprouts that are cooked golden brown and then seared in
beef fat with the flambadou. A fruity grilled plum sauce is a perfect complement.

**Serves 2 as part of a
multi-course menu**

3 Brussels sprouts
2 teaspoons butter
1 x 15g piece of beef fat or
    tallow from dry-aged beef
    (page 288)
sea salt

For the smoked parsley root
1 parsley root/Hamburg
    parsley (mature, not
    too young)

For the plum sauce
4 plums

Peel the parsley root and cut off the ends. Cook in lightly salted boiling
water for 2 minutes. Drain and cool down in iced water. Hot smoke the
parsley root for 10 hours every day for 1–2 weeks until it is dried out.

Cut the plums in half and remove the stones. Place the plums, cut side
down, on a rack set over a medium heat and grill until golden brown. Turn
the plums and keep grilling until soft in the centre. Put the grilled plums
into a blender or small food processor and blitz to a smooth paste. Pass
through a fine sieve into a saucepan. Bring to the boil over a medium heat
and reduce the plum paste to a creamy consistency. Leave to cool.

Rinse the Brussels sprouts and cut each one in half. Heat a frying pan over
a medium heat and sear the sprouts in the butter until golden brown on all
sides, but still firm in the middle.

Arrange the Brussels sprout halves, cut side up, on an untreated wood
plank. Sear each sprout for 6–8 seconds with burning beef fat from
the flambadou.

Using a microplane, grate the smoked parsley root on top of the Brussels
sprouts and serve warm with the plum sauce on the side.

Langoustine, charcoal cream & cold-smoked parsnip

152

Langoustines seared with burning beef fat, served with burning birch wood-infused rich cream thickened with ättika and a smoky parsnip.

**Serves 1 as a middle course
or 2 as a snack**

1 parsnip
2 langoustine tails
a branch of fresh pine
1 x 15g piece of beef fat or
   tallow from dry-aged beef
   (page 288)
30g Charcoal Cream
   (page 286), to serve
sea salt

Peel the parsnip and cut off the ends. Cook in lightly salted boiling water for 1 minute, then drain and immediately cool down in iced water. Cold smoke with birch wood for 2 hours.

Peel the langoustine tails. Straighten out each tail and put it on a skewer. Hot smoke with fresh pine for 1–2 minutes.

Place the langoustines on an untreated wood plank and sear each tail for 8–10 seconds with burning beef fat from the flambadou.

Remove the skewers and cut each langoustine tail into 3 pieces. Serve with charcoal cream and a thin slice of cold-smoked parsnip. Serve semi-warm.

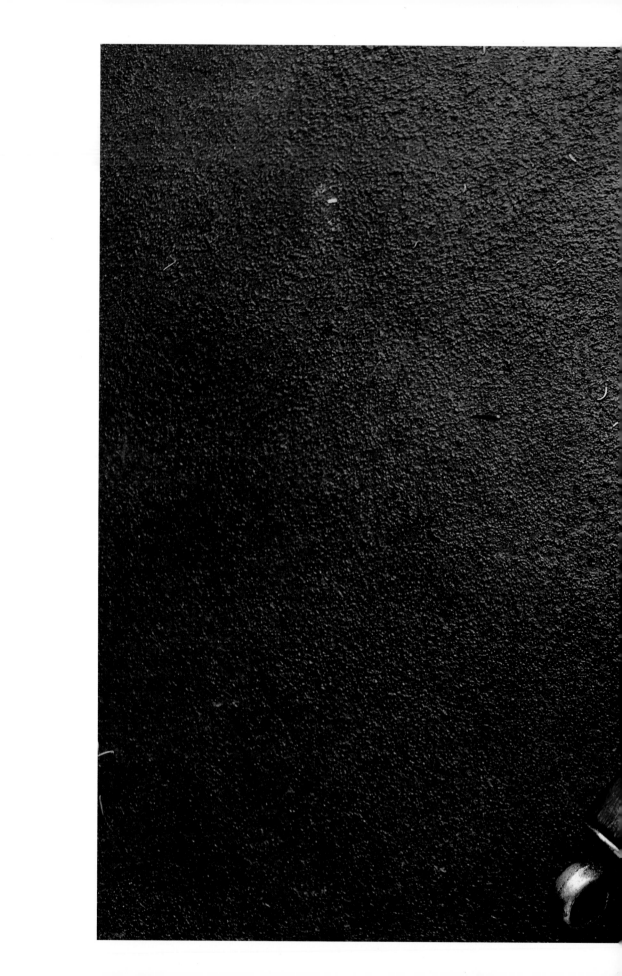

Scallop & coral sabayon

Flambadou
Autumn / Winter

Flambadou-cooked scallops served with a foamy sabayon seasoned
with scallop coral.

Serves 4 as a snack

2 fresh scallops in their shells
30g unsalted butter
1 x 15g piece of beef fat or
 tallow from dry-aged beef
 (page 288)
sea salt

For the sabayon
40ml Vegetable Stock
 (page 278)
2 egg yolks

Carefully open each scallop shell and take out the white muscle (the
scallop) and the coral. Clean them and discard the guts. Save the bottom
shells. Reserve the corals for the sabayon.

Sear the scallops in the butter in a cast-iron pan for 1–2 minutes on each
side. Remove from the heat.

Combine the corals with the vegetable stock and egg yolks in a saucepan
(or a large heatproof bowl). Add a pinch of salt. Mix until smooth using
a stick blender. Set the saucepan over a medium heat (or the bowl over a
pan of simmering water) and whisk constantly until the sabayon is thick
and smooth.

Place the scallops on an untreated wood plank and sear each one for
6–8 seconds with burning beef fat from the flambadou. Cut each scallop
in half, season with sea salt and serve with the warm coral sabayon.

Flambadou Arctic char & crispy skin

158

This beautiful cold-water fish lives further north than any other freshwater fish
Its colour varies, depending on the time of year and the environment it lives in.
For this dish we cook the skin and fillet separately to make the skin really crispy.

Serves 2 as a snack

1 x 400g fillet of Arctic char
(skin on), pin-boned
½ tablespoon rapeseed oil
1 x 15g piece of beef fat or
tallow from dry-aged beef
(page 288)
sea salt

Sprinkle the char fillet with ½ teaspoon salt, then leave at room
temperature for 30 minutes. Rinse in cold water and pat dry with
kitchen towel.

Place the fillet in a smoker, skin side up. Smoke at 35–40°C until the
fillet reaches an internal temperature of 35°C. Remove from the smoker.
Carefully remove the skin in one piece. Set the fillet aside.

Preheat the oven to 60°C.

Brush the skin with the oil and season with ½ teaspoon salt. Lay the
skin out flat in a cold ovenproof frying pan. Place over a low heat initially
and gently heat to a medium-high heat, then sear for 2–3 minutes to dry
out. Remove the pan from the heat and place it in the oven to dry the skin
for about 2 hours until crispy.

Cut the fillet into 4 pieces and place on an untreated wood plank. Sear each
piece for 6–8 seconds with burning beef fat from the flambadou.

Divide the skin into 4 pieces and top with the char. Season with a pinch
of sea salt and serve.

Flamed Jerusalem artichokes with sunflower seed emulsion

Flambadou
Autumn / Winter

160

A typical winter-season dish with mature Jerusalem artichokes and roasted sunflower seeds.

Serves 4

4 Jerusalem artichokes, about 10–15cm in size
1 tablespoon butter
1 x 15g piece of beef fat or tallow from dry-aged beef (page 288)
Sunflower Seed Emulsion (page 281), to serve

Place the artichokes in the flames and leave for about 30 minutes until cooked through and soft in the middle. Remove from the fire and leave to cool, then brush clean of ash.

Cut each artichoke in half lengthways. Sear in the butter in a frying pan over a medium heat until golden brown. Remove from the heat.

Place the artichoke halves, skin side down, on an untreated wood plank. Sear each artichoke for 6–8 seconds with burning beef fat from the flambadou. Serve warm with sunflower seed emulsion.

Reindeer heart, burnt nut oil & yellow pea sauce

162

The Sami always use every part of a reindeer, even the heart. In Sweden we also have a long tradition of dishes made with deer, venison and moose heart. The heart is most commonly brined and warm-smoked to be served as charcuterie.

Serves 4 as a snack

200g reindeer heart
½ tablespoon sea salt
1 x 15g piece of beef fat or tallow from dry-aged beef (page 288)
1 tablespoon yellow pea sauce (page 289)
3 tablespoons frozen lingonberries (page 288), thawed

For the burnt nut oil
1 tablespoon sesame seeds
200ml rapeseed oil

Clean the reindeer heart, removing any sinews and fat. Combine the salt and 500ml water, whisking to dissolve the salt. Add the heart and leave to brine for 20 minutes. Drain on kitchen paper.

To make the oil, roast the sesame seeds in a pan over a medium-high heat until golden brown. Blitz with the oil in a blender to a smooth paste. Strain through a sieve. (Leftover oil can be kept at room temperature for 3 months; use it in a salad dressing with vinegar or lemon juice.)

Place the reindeer heart on an untreated wooden plank. Sear for 5 seconds with burning beef fat from the flambadou.

Cut the heart into thin slices, 4 or 5 per portion. Top with the yellow pea sauce, a drizzle of nut oil and the lingonberries.

Spring/
Summer

In Lofoten

Legendary Lofoten

170

I visited Lofoten in Scandinavia for the first time only a couple of years ago. A Norwegian tv show had asked me to come to Lofoten to cook cod, or skrei, on air, and although I'd had the scenery described to me and seen photos from the fjords beforehand, I couldn't possibly imagine how incredibly beautiful and magical this place would turn out to be.

I remember I arrived late in the evening. The air was crisp and clear, as it always is in Lofoten; it never gets warm here, not even in summer. It must have been April or May and since it was spring, the sun hadn't set completely when I arrived. However, it was still too dark to take in the surroundings properly, so I checked into my hotel and went to bed. In the morning I opened the curtains, only to be gobsmacked by this stunning view of steep, snow-clad mountains literally diving into the glittering sea. It was love at first sight.

This extraordinary nature, so raw and untouched by man, bore a natural crudeness that swept me off my feet in a way I was totally unprepared for. Ever since, I've been back at least twice a year to fish, hike or stay with friends I've come to know on this incredible peninsula. Every time I return, I get to discover something new: a new bay, a new village, a new mountain – or a familiar mountain seen in a different light or from a different angle.

Fishing

In Lofoten
Spring / Summer

Lofoten is characterised by fishing, especially fishing for skrei, a cod fish from the Barents Sea that migrates down past Lofoten every spring. One could call it an 'athletic cod' as it is exceptionally fast and slender due to having swum such long distances in extremely cold water. In the early days, small fishing boats came up from southern Norway to catch enormous amounts of fish, and the trade was notoriously hard and harsh – and still is, although it has been modernised. Today the skrei industry is strictly regulated by the Norwegian government, to ensure the fish stock isn't depleted.

The vast majority of the permanent residents in Lofoten are extremely hard working, often having two jobs or more – one in fishing and one in tourism. I've come to love and respect the coarse and, at the same time, pure and natural atmosphere I sense and associate with the dramatic scenery and the people who live here. To lead a life in this dark, austere part of Scandinavia during the winter months builds a very strong character, but I often find that conversations – as well as the comments I get for what I do – are genuinely warm and cordial.

Nature's bounty

In Lofoten
Spring / Summer

However inspiring I find Lofoten, my returning as often as possible has nothing to do with learning any sophisticated or intriguing cooking techniques, but rather stems from my fascination for the exquisite raw materials, for which I have come to grow an everlasting love and respect. For me, every trip to Lofoten is a personal adventure and a way to feel truly connected to nature, but also a way to celebrate and highlight sustainability and nature's own amazing resources.

The Lofoten stockfish

Freshly caught skrei is a real treat, but the fish is unbelievably tasty even when dried, which is a very common way of preservation. The Norwegian name for the dried fish meat is *tørrfisk*, but in southern Europe and South America the skrei is more commonly known by the beautiful name *bacalao*. It is a very popular ingredient in Latin America, Portugal and Spain, where it's often served with tomato sauce. Surprisingly, the fish heads are exported to Africa, and dried skrei heads are a common feature there, especially in Nigerian kitchens. It all started in the 1960s, when Norwegian fishermen realised that the fish heads – which were often thrown away – could be sent to those living in starving countries, who quickly saw the benefits of the highly nutritious heads. Skrei-based soups became everyday food, and still, several decades later, fish meal (made from ground, dried skrei heads) is a common ingredient in many popular African dishes.

Personally, I prefer my skrei, or *bacalao*, served as it is. The time I've spent in Lofoten has made me take skrei to my heart, and I make sure to use it whenever in season. Actually, I'm a fan of *tørrfisk* too and often cook it for the kids at home. There's something meaty and rich about it, which in my opinion makes skrei the finest fish money can buy.

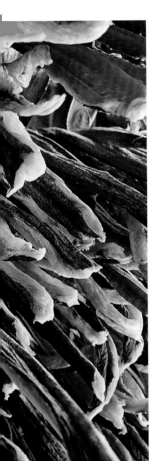

The scenery

In Lofoten
Spring / Summer

184

Lofoten is an incredibly scenic place to visit. Tiny fishing villages with beautiful architecture are scattered along the coastline, making the peninsula a perfect location for exploration. Lately, tourism has become an important business in this part of Norway, hence the increasing number of hotels and hostels available to the public and not just to the fishermen. Hiking, angling or just enjoying the extraordinary mountain views are becoming more and more popular among tourists from all over the world. However, the one thing you can never be sure of is the weather. It comes and goes and changes incredibly fast, something I myself have experienced several times; one minute the starlight evening sky is crisp and clear, the next the wind is howling with rain banging on the windowpane – it may even snow! It sometimes feels like you experience three or four seasons within just two days, which of course adds to Lofoten's charm and uniqueness.

Although I always enjoy a day out fishing, in my opinion the most beautiful part of Lofoten is the famous hiking trails. The dramatic and untainted beauty of a shoreline consisting entirely of steep mountains is breath-taking and never fails to fascinate me.

And I'm not alone – Lofoten has become a well-known destination on Instagram. Many a thousand selfies and photos of the fjord have entranced the digital world. I've been to places where I've ended up slightly disappointed that the scenery didn't live up to my expectations, but Lofoten is better than images seen in books or on Instagram feeds. The setting is so unique and overwhelming that, unless you're a professional photographer, it's almost not worth picking up your camera – the photo will never capture the essence and impressiveness of the untouched brutality, the relentless, raw cold and the harsh climate.

Wood Oven

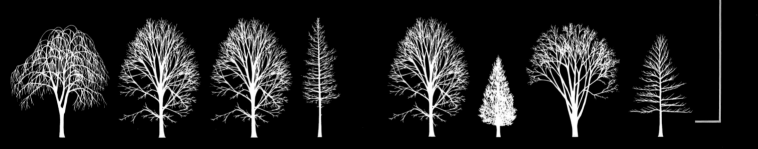

Spring cabbages with black garlic & cabbage broth

Wood Oven

Spring / Summer

Spring and early summer is the season for young and delicate cabbages. In this recipe we've used a variety of cooking techniques for different kinds of cabbage and added an emulsion of fermented garlic.

Serves 4 as a middle course

Black Garlic Emulsion
  (page 281), to serve
salt

For the cabbage broth
250g finely chopped green
  cabbage
30g butter
1 litre Vegetable Stock
  (page 278)

For the roast Chinese leaves
1 head Chinese leaves, about
  600g
30g Smoked Butter (page 285)

For the roast Brussels sprouts
4 Brussels sprouts, halved
1 tablespoon Clarified Butter
  (page 284)

*For the hot-smoked red
  cabbage*
1 x 200g wedge red cabbage
15g Smoked Butter (page 285)

*For the ember-cooked green
  cabbage*
2 large outside leaves of green
  cabbage
10g Smoked Butter (page 285)

For the romanesco
2 romanesco florets
1 tablespoon Clarified Butter
  (page 284)

For the fried cavolo nero
2 large leaves cavolo nero
3 tablespoons Clarified Butter
  (page 284)

For the broth, fry the chopped cabbage in the butter in a wide pan over a medium-high heat until soft and shiny. Lower the heat and keep frying until the cabbage is golden brown and has a sweet caramelised aroma. Add the vegetable stock, increase the heat and bring to the boil. Leave to simmer until reduced to about 400ml. Strain the broth through a sieve and season with salt. Reheat for serving.

Cut the head of Chinese leaves into quarters lengthways. Rub with 1 tablespoon salt. Set aside at room temperature for 30 minutes.

Preheat the oven to 180°C. Rinse the Chinese leaves in cold water and drain well. Place on a baking tray and roast for about 30 minutes until cooked through in the centre: check with a skewer or paring knife. Remove from the oven and brush with the smoked butter. Set aside; reheat for serving.

Mix the Brussels sprouts with the clarified butter on a small baking tray. Roast in the oven for 15–20 minutes, until golden brown but still firm in the centre. Season with salt. Set aside; reheat for serving.

Cut the wedge of red cabbage into quarters and blanch in lightly salted boiling water for about 40 seconds. Cool down in iced water. Drain well, place on a tray and hot smoke for 5 minutes. Remove from the smoker and brush with the smoked butter.

Slice the green cabbage leaves thinly and blanch in lightly salted boiling water for 20 seconds. Cool down in iced water. Drain well and place in a wide metal sieve. Place the sieve on top of the embers and 'sauté' for 1–2 minutes. Add the smoked butter, stir and allow it to melt into the cabbage. Remove from the heat. Set aside; reheat for serving.

Cut the romanesco florets in half vertically. Blanch in lightly salted boiling water for about 20 seconds. Cool down in iced water, then fry with the clarified butter in a pan and set aside.

Cut out the stem from the cavolo nero leaves. Fry the leaves with the clarified butter in a wide pan, keeping the leaves flat. Cook until crispy. Remove from the heat and drain on kitchen paper. Season with salt.

To serve, divide the Chinese leaves, Brussels sprouts and red cabbage among the plates. Top with green cabbage, romanesco and crispy cavolo nero. Serve with black garlic emulsion and the cabbage broth.

Redfish collar, fish sauce & fried nettles

Next time you are at your local fishmonger I suggest you ask for a collar, which is the bony triangle of tender, fatty meat tucked between the fish's gills and the rest of its body. I find it to be a great part of the fish for barbecue. And it is cheap, because it's a throwaway cut that not many ask for. Keep it simple and serve it with fish sauce and some nettles. I recommend you eat this with your hands or chopsticks as a sharing dish.

Serves 2–4 as a snack

1–2 redfish collars, 100–200g in total
15g Smoked Butter (page 285)
1 teaspoon ättika (page 288)
2 tablespoons Hay Salt (page 283)
sea salt

For the fish sauce
400g whole herrings (or sardines or mackerel)
2 garlic cloves, peeled
8 black peppercorns
3 bay leaves

For the fried nettles
a bunch of nettle leaves
2 tablespoons cooking oil

To make the fish sauce, cut the whole fish into pieces and pack into a large jar. Mash the fish with a potato masher or mortar. Add the garlic, peppercorns, bay leaves, 100g sea salt and enough water to cover the fish completely. Mix well. Cover the jar tightly with a lid and leave to ferment in a cold, dark place for 1–3 months. For the first few weeks, 'burp' the jar (remove the lid briefly) every few days – preferably outside!– to prevent pressure from building up.

Strain the contents through a fine-mesh sieve into a glass bowl and set aside to settle for 30 minutes. Pour the cloudy brown liquid through a coffee filter – it will take some time to filter through. (It's a good idea to do this outside because of the smell.)

Properly stored (in a tightly covered jar in a cool place), fish sauce will keep for many months, or even years if stored in the fridge.

Pick 10 nettle leaves and rinse in cold water. Drain well on kitchen paper. Heat the oil in a pan and fry the nettles for about 30 seconds until crispy. Drain on kitchen paper. Season with salt.

Preheat the oven to 180°C. Rub the collars with ½ teaspoon salt and roast for 12–15 minutes until cooked all the way through. Brush with the smoked butter when serving.

Serve the collars with 50ml of your home-made fish sauce mixed with the ättika, crispy nettles and hay salt.

Braised lamb shoulder, seaweed butter, greens & wild garlic capers

198

Here a slow-cooked, tender lamb shoulder is served with seaweed butter, which gives it a salty aroma of the sea, as well as salty, tart wild garlic capers, spicy mustard greens and jus.

Serves 4 as a main course

1 lamb shoulder, about 500g
400–800ml Chicken Stock
   (page 279) or water
1 tablespoon Wild Garlic
   Capers (page 281)
sea salt

For the seaweed butter
2 tablespoons Home-made
   Butter (page 284), at room
   temperature
1 teaspoon dried seaweed
   (page 288)

For the seared beans
20 fresh sprouted broad
   beans or mung beans
½ tablespoon butter

*For the butter-seared wild
   garlic leaves*
8 wild garlic leaves
2 tablespoons Clarified
   Butter (page 284)

For the greens
a bunch of mustard greens
a bunch of golden frill (kale
   or mustard cross)
1 tablespoon cold-pressed
   rapeseed oil

Preheat the oven to 130°C.

Bone the lamb shoulder and season with well with salt. Roll up and tie with kitchen string to make an even bolster shape. Sear all over in a pan over a medium-high heat for 1–2 minutes on each side. Transfer the lamb to a roasting tin. Add enough chicken stock (or water) to come halfway up the side of the lamb. Cover with foil and braise in the oven for 2½ hours until tender in the centre: check with a skewer or paring knife. Remove from the oven. Lift the lamb on to a carving board and set aside to rest for 30 minutes.

Boil the braising jus in the tin to reduce by half. Season with salt.

Combine the butter and dried seaweed and mix thoroughly.

Sear the beans quickly in the butter in a small pan over a high heat, about 15 seconds.

Rinse the wild garlic leaves in cold water and drain on kitchen paper. Sear in a wide pan with the clarified butter, making sure to keep the leaves flat, for 10–15 seconds on each side. Drain on kitchen paper. Season with salt.

Combine all the ingredients for the greens and mix well, then add the seared beans and a pinch of salt.

Untie the lamb and cut into 4 portions. Spread a spoonful of seaweed butter in the middle of each plate. Place the lamb in the centre of the plate and top with the greens and beans mixture, butter-seared wild garlic leaves and wild garlic capers. Serve with the reduced braising jus.

Saffron pancake, birch syrup & juniper-infused vodka

Wood Oven
Spring / Summer

200

Swedish pancakes, called 'plättar', are about 8cm in diameter and cooked in a special cast-iron pan with four to seven moulds, which is called a 'plättjärn'. We season our pancakes with saffron and flame them with juniper-infused vodka, then serve them with birch sap reduced to a sweet syrup.

**Serves 4 as a dessert or
'fika' (coffee snack)**

For the juniper-infused vodka
750ml vodka
a branch of juniper, fresh
  and green

For the saffron pancakes
140ml whole milk
2g saffron threads
1 egg
1 tablespoon caster sugar
90g plain flour
butter, for frying

To serve
2 tablespoons birch syrup
  (page 288)

Combine the vodka and branch of juniper in a bottle or jar. Cover and leave at room temperature for 30 days before using. (The juniper-infused vodka can be kept for years.)

Heat the milk to 37°C (finger warm) and add the saffron. Cover with a lid and leave to infuse, off the heat, for 30 minutes.

Pour the milk into a bowl and add the egg, sugar, flour and 40ml water. Whisk to a smooth batter.

Melt a little butter in a 'plättjärn' (see page 289), or Scotch pancake pan, on a medium-high heat. Add the batter to make 4 or 8 pancakes and leave until the butter is browned and the pancakes are cooked through. Add 60ml juniper-infused vodka and set it alight. Remove from the heat and let the flames burn down. Pour over the birch syrup, stir and serve.

If you're making ahead of time, cook the pancakes and then set aside. When you're ready to serve, melt a little more butter in the pan and reheat the pancakes, then add the vodka and proceed as above.

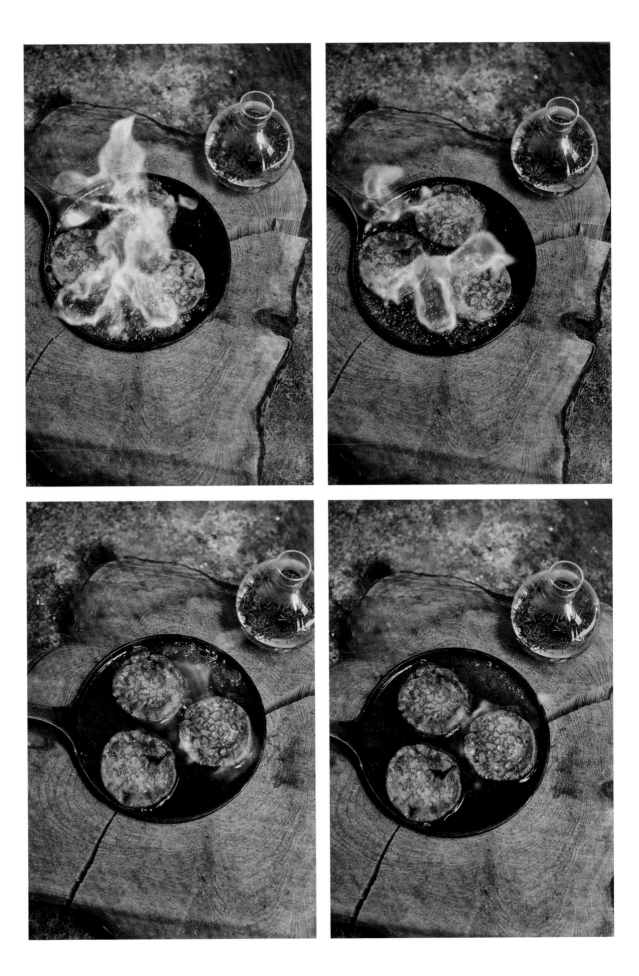

Baked almond cake & grilled unripe strawberries

Wood Oven

Spring / Summer

A really simple and traditional cake recipe, but so tasty. It is quite sweet, so is well balanced by tart unripened green strawberries. Strawberries are something really special in Sweden, synonymous with a good summer. You will see pick-your-own farms and pop-up stands along roads selling strawberries. People talk about the year's quality and price, and always praise Swedish strawberries as the best.

Serves 4 as a dessert

butter, for greasing
100ml Strawberry Purée
   (page 287)
4 sweet cecily leaves

For the almond cakes
75g unsalted butter, at room
   temperature, plus extra for
   greasing
150g Almond Paste
   (page 287)
75g eggs

For the strawberry sorbet
2 gelatine leaves
300ml Stock Syrup
   (page 286)
500ml Strawberry Purée
   (page 287)

For the grilled strawberries
4–6 white or green unripe
   strawberries

Preheat the oven to 180°C. Line the bottom of 4 portion-sized cake tins with baking parchment, then grease the paper and the sides of the tins with the butter.

Beat the butter and almond paste to a smooth consistency. Keep beating while you add the eggs, one at a time. Scoop the mixture into the tins – the mix should be about 3cm deep. Place in the oven and bake for 15–20 minutes until risen and golden brown, and a skewer inserted into the centre comes out clean. Remove from the oven and cool in the tins for 15 minutes before turning out on to a wire rack. Leave to cool completely.

To make the sorbet, soak the gelatine in cold water for 15 minutes. Heat up half of the syrup until just warm. Squeeze excess water from the gelatine, then add to the warm syrup and stir to melt. Combine the strawberry purée with the gelatine mixture and the remaining syrup. Churn in an ice cream machine. (Any sorbet not used for this recipe can be kept in the freezer.)

Grill the strawberries on 2 sides over a high heat to make grill stripes. Cool down in the fridge for 15 minutes. Slice thinly using a sharp thin knife.

To assemble, arrange the grilled strawberry slices around the edges of each almond cake. Put a spoonful of strawberry purée in the centre of each plate and place an almond cake on the purée. Top each cake with a quenelle of strawberry sorbet and a sweet cecily leaf.

Oat cake, blackcurrant & birch ice cream

Wood Oven

Spring / Summer

Infusing the flavour of birch into food was something we worked on for a long time. Birch is such an important part of our cooking – every day ten to fifteen bags of birch wood have to be chopped at Ekstedt, to get fuel for the kitchen. With this infusing technique we were able to get the flavour of the tree into the ice cream. It's almost like a vanilla pod and also gives a beautiful aroma. We serve the ice cream with a light oat-flour cake and blackcurrants, which many people have growing at home in their garden.

Serves 4 as a dessert

For the oat cakes
2 eggs
100g caster sugar
60g oat flour
80g unsalted butter, melted

For the birch ice cream
500ml double cream
500ml whole milk
120g caster sugar
10 birchwood sticks
6 egg yolks

*For the blackcurrant
  leaf crisps*
4 young blackcurrant leaves
100g sugar
1 tablespoon blackcurrant
  leaf powder (page 288)

To serve
150ml blackcurrants

Preheat the oven to 180°C.

Whisk the eggs with the sugar to an airy and smooth consistency. Fold in the flour. Keep stirring and slowly pour in the melted butter. Divide the mixture among 4 silicone moulds that are 6–8cm diameter – the mix should be about 2cm deep. Bake for about 10 minutes until the cakes are risen and golden brown, and a skewer inserted into the centre comes out clean. Cool down for a couple of minutes, then turn out onto a wire rack and leave to cool completely.

Combine the cream, milk, 50g of the sugar and the birchwood sticks in a wide pan and bring to the boil over a medium-high heat. Remove from the heat, cover with a lid and leave to infuse for 30 minutes.

Combine the remaining sugar with the egg yolks in a heavy-based saucepan (or in a double boiler or bowl set over a pan of hot water). Strain in the birchwood-infused liquid and stir to dissolve the sugar. Cook over a medium-high heat, constantly stirring with a spatula over the bottom of the pan, until a creamy consistency (85°C). Remove from the heat and pour the custard into a bowl placed on ice to cool down quickly. Churn in an ice cream machine.

Heat the oven to 75°C. Rinse the blackcurrant leaves in cold water and drain on kitchen paper. Heat the sugar with 100ml water, stirring until the sugar has dissolved. Dip the leaves in the syrup and place on a silicone mat on a baking tray. Dry in the oven for 6–10 hours (keep the oven door slightly ajar to avoid humidity).

To assemble and serve, cover the oat cakes with fresh blackcurrants. Top each cake with a quenelle of birch ice cream. Sprinkle blackcurrant powder over the crispy leaves and place on the ice cream.

Smoked

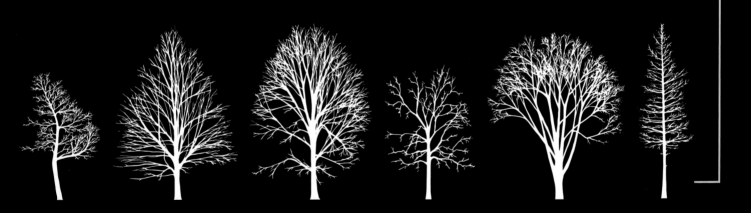

Cold-smoked halibut, samphire & asparagus

We use whey for its acidity, like using wine for cooking. Here we poach green asparagus in whey to add some acidity to the plate with cold-smoked halibut and a samphire cream.

Serves 4 as a middle course

180g halibut loin
sea salt

*For the samphire
    soured cream*
120g soured cream
30g samphire

*For the grilled whey-cooked
    green asparagus*
8 green asparagus spears
100ml whey (page 289)

To serve
12 samphire spears
8 rapeseed flowers (page 289)

Drain the soured cream in a coffee filter set over a bowl for 2 hours. Juice the samphire, or blitz to a purée and pass through a sieve. Combine with the drained soured cream, stirring to a smooth consistency.

Combine 5 tablespoons salt with 1 litre water in a flat dish, whisking to dissolve the salt. Place the halibut in this brine and set aside for 20 minutes. Remove from the brine and dry with kitchen paper. Cold smoke for 20 minutes. Remove from the smoker and leave to rest in the fridge for 20 minutes. Slice into 8 pieces.

Cut off the tough end of the stem from each asparagus spear. Place the spears in a pan and half cover with the whey. Add ½ teaspoon salt and poach over a medium-high heat for 1 minute. Remove from the liquid and drain on kitchen paper. Grill over embers for 2 minutes on each side until golden brown.

Place the asparagus in the centre of the plates. Curl the fish slices on top and add the samphire soured cream on the side. Top with the samphire spears and rapeseed flowers.

Smoked vendace roe, potatoes & ash soured cream

Vendace roe is Swedish caviar. It comes from the vendace, a fish in the Salmonidae family found in fresh water and in brackish water, such as in the north Baltic Sea. Lightly and freshly smoking the roe just before serving adds a delicate aroma. Served with ember-baked potato, pickled cucumber and ash-infused sour cream, we recommend you enjoy it with a cold lager and chilled aquavit.

Serves 4 as a middle course

160g vendace roe (page 289)
1 teaspoon Hay Ash
   (page 283)

For the pickled cucumber
1 large cucumber
100ml ättika (page 288)
100g sugar
1 teaspoon sea salt

For the ember-baked potato
250g potatoes (last season's
   tasty potatoes, stored over
   the winter to mature),
   unpeeled

For the ash soured cream
4 tablespoons soured cream
1 teaspoon Hay Ash
   (page 283)

Slice the cucumber vertically to give 4 'sides', not including the seeded centre. Combine the ättika, sugar, salt and 200ml water in a bowl. Whisk to dissolve the sugar and salt. Add the cucumber and set aside to pickle for 20 minutes. Drain on kitchen paper.

Arrange the cucumber pieces on a sheet of baking parchment on a cutting board, slightly overlapping them. Using a round mould or cutter 6–8cm in diameter, stamp out 4 rounds of cucumber.

Cold smoke the vendace roe for 30 seconds. Repeat a further 1 or 2 times until the roe has a lightly smoky aroma.

Place the potatoes in the embers and scoop up more embers to cover the potatoes. Cook for 25–40 minutes, turning the potatoes every 10 minutes, until they are soft in the centre: check with a paring knife or skewer. Remove from the fire and cool down to room temperature. Cut open the potatoes and scoop out the flesh.

Combine the soured cream and hay ash.

In the centre of each plate, spread the potato flesh and ash soured cream in the same round shape as the cucumber. Cover with the cucumber rounds and sprinkle with hay ash. Top each with a quenelle of smoked vendace roe.

Juniper-smoked pike-perch, chicory & whey

This dish has the feel of early spring, a time before the first baby salad and leaves are ready for the season. Chicory grown underground or indoors in the absence of sunlight prevents the leaves from turning green and opening up. This makes it possible to harvest the chicory very early and adds a freshness to the dish. Cooking the chicory in whey balances the bitterness perfectly. Pike-perch is a freshwater fish common in lakes in the region around Stockholm and is similar in taste to its related 'fish-brother', perch.

Serves 4 as a main course

4 x 120g pieces of pike-perch (zander) fillet, skin on
15g butter
a branch of juniper
2 tablespoons Juniper Butter (page 285)
4 winter purslane leaves, to garnish

For the whey-braised chicory
1 head chicory
300ml whey (page 289)
½ teaspoon sea salt

For the juniper-infused whey fish sauce
100ml Fish Stock (page 278)
3 tablespoons Juniper Butter (page 285)

Cut the chicory into quarters lengthways. Place in a pan and cover with the whey. Add the salt. Simmer gently for 4–6 minutes until tender but still firm in the centre. Drain, reserving the whey.

Sear the pike-perch on the skin side in the butter in a hot cast-iron pan for 2–3 minutes until golden brown. Turn the fish over carefully and remove from the heat. Place the branch of juniper on top of the fish. Set the juniper alight and cover the pan with a lid or bowl to kill the fire. Set aside, covered, for 3 minutes to smoke.

Combine the fish stock and 50ml of the reserved whey in a saucepan, bring to the boil and simmer to reduce to about 100ml.

Sear the chicory quickly in a really hot cast-iron pan.

Just before serving, heat up the sauce and add the juniper butter. Mix together with a stick blender.

Brush the fish with the juniper butter and place in the centre of the plates with the chicory alongside. Place a good spoonful of the sauce on each plate and garnish with a leaf of winter purslane.

Smoked seaweed-brined sea bream & consommé

216

When oyster are delivered to Ekstedt, they are packed in bladderwrack seawood. In this recipe they are used for fish consommé. Seaweed brings a natural saltiness and it is great for brining fish.

Serves 4 as a main course

4 sheets dried nori or kelp, each about 10 x 20cm
300ml Fish Stock (page 278)
4 x 120g portions sea bream fillet, skin on
cooking oil
160g seaweed salad (page 289)

For the fish consommé
a bunch of fresh bladderwrack seaweed, chopped (about 200ml)
500g pike or pike-perch (zander) flesh
2 sprigs of thyme, leaves picked
1 bay leaf
8 tarragon leaves
5 egg whites
1.5 litres Fish Stock (page 278)

Simmer the nori/kelp in the stock for 20 minutes. Remove the nori/kelp and cool down. Set the stock aside. Drain the kelp on kitchen towel and cold smoke for 10 minutes.

Wrap the portions of sea bream individually in the nori/kelp. Set aside in the fridge for 1½ hours.

To make the consommé, rinse the seaweed in running cold water for 5 minutes. Using a mincer or food processor, grind the pike flesh with the seaweed, thyme leaves, bay leaf and tarragon. Combine the ground ingredients with the egg whites in a stockpot. Add the cold fish stock together with the reserved kelp-infused stock.

Set the pot over a medium-high heat and stir carefully until simmering – it's important to stir to prevent the fish mixture from sticking and burning at the bottom of the pot. Once simmering, the fish mixture will float up to the surface. Allow it to coagulate, then make a little hole in the centre, about 5cm wide, and carefully scoop some warm stock over the surface to make sure it has all coagulated. Simmer for about 45 minutes.

Remove from the heat and leave to cool for 30 minutes. Strain through a muslin-lined sieve – the fish mixture will have gathered up all the impurities and the consommé will be clear. (Any leftover consommé can be kept in the fridge for 3 days or frozen.)

Unwrap the fish and drain skin side down on kitchen paper. Brush the skin with cooking oil, then sear the fish on the skin side in a hot pan for 2–3 minutes until almost cooked through. Remove from the pan to a tray, placing the fish skin side up. Leave to rest for a minute.

Steam or blanch the seaweed salad to heat up. Place in the centre of soup plates and top with the pieces of fish. Ladle some warm consommé around.

Smoked 'kalvdans' & cloudberries

'Kalvdans' is our Swedish version of crema catalana or crème brûlée. It has a long history in Swedish cuisine, with recipes dating from 1682. Traditionally it was made from the first milk after the cows give birth when the milk is so rich in protein. Unfortunately, 'kalvdans' is rarely made today, as very few families keep cows of their own and it is not always easy to find colostrum. But it is worth giving it a try.

Serves 4 as a dessert

For the cloudberry compote
200g cloudberries (page 288)
100g caster sugar
2 tablespoons pine shoots
(page 289)
3g pectin powder

Rinse the cloudberries and remove any stems. Combine the cloudberries and sugar in a saucepan and bring to the boil over a medium-low heat. Simmer for 4 minutes. Add the pine shoots and simmer for a further minute. Remove from the heat, add the pectin powder and stir well. Cool down to room temperature, stirring every 5 minutes. (Any leftover compote can be kept in the fridge for 1 month.)

For the 'kalvdans'
400ml fresh bovine
colostrum (page 288)
2 tablespoons caster sugar
2 tablespoons brown sugar

Pour the colostrum and caster sugar into a saucepan and heat to dissolve the sugar. Cold smoke for 10 minutes.

Preheat the oven to 110°C. Pour the smoked colostrum into 4 portion-sized cocottes or other oven-proof dishes. Set the dishes in a roasting tin of water and bake for 45 minutes until set. Remove from the oven and leave to cool.

Sprinkle a thin layer of brown sugar on top of the baked colostrum cocottes. Use a kitchen blowtorch to melt and caramelise the brown sugar. Serve with cloudberry compote.

Seasonal berries, smoked syrup, rye tuile & cheesecake

220

This dish was inspired by a typical dessert that we would eat at our summer house using fresh berries picked in the garden. You can vary this with whatever berries are in season, farmed or foraged, such as cloudberries or wild strawberries.

Serves 4 as a dessert

200g seasonal berries
 (strawberries, raspberries,
 red/black currants, dessert
 gooseberries)
12 edible flowers in season

For the smoked syrup
150g granulated sugar

For the rye tuile
65g unsalted butter
50g honey
50g rye flour

For the cheesecake
3 gelatine leaves
250ml double cream
5 tablespoons sugar
150g cream cheese, at
 room temperature

To make the syrup, combine the sugar and 100ml water in a pan and bring to the boil, whisking to dissolve the sugar. Hot smoke for 10 minutes. Strain through a fine sieve. Set aside to cool. (Leftover syrup can be stored in a dry, cold place for up to 1 month.)

Preheat the oven to 175°C.

Melt the butter with the honey in a saucepan. Remove from the heat, add the rye flour and stir to a smooth paste. Cool down to room temperature. Spread out the paste in a thin (2mm) layer on a silicone sheet and bake for 3–4 minutes until golden brown. Cool on the silicone sheet. When set, break into 4 portions.

Soak the gelatine in cold water for 20 minutes. Heat up 50ml of the cream with the sugar; remove from the heat. Squeeze any excess water from the gelatine, then add to the warm cream and whisk to melt. Add the cream cheese and whisk to a smooth consistency. Whip the remaining cream lightly, then fold into the cream cheese mixture. Place in a piping bag.

Rinse the berries and remove any stems. Cut larger berries in half. Combine with 2 tablespoons of the smoked syrup, folding together gently.

Pipe out the cheesecake into 4 bowls on top of the rye tuile. Spoon the berries on to the cheesecake. Garnish with edible flowers.

Ember

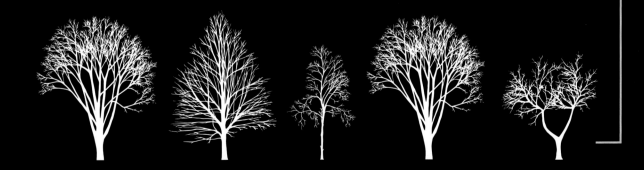

Knäckebröd with sorrel spread & radishes

224

Small red radishes grow really fast and can be ready for the first harvest in late spring or early summer, which is really exciting after a long winter. Crispy, tasty and a bit spicy.

Serves 4 as a snack

2 red radishes, thinly sliced
2 tablespoons garden cress
sea salt

For the knäckebröd
  (see page 288)

Step 1
30g butter
1 tablespoon honey
5g fresh yeast
150ml milk
100g rye flour
100g strong wheat flour

Step 2
200g almond potatoes
  (page 288)
100g graham flour (coarse-
  ground wholemeal flour)
100g strong wheat flour

For the sorrel spread
15 sorrel leaves
3 tablespoons Grilled Onion
  Greens Paste (see recipe
  for Turbot on the Bone and
  Onion Variations,
  page 232)

For the butter-fried sorrel
4 sorrel leaves
1 tablespoon Clarified Butter
  (page 284)

For step 1 of the knäckebröd, melt the butter in a saucepan, then add the honey, yeast and milk. Heat up to finger warmth to dissolve the honey and yeast. Pour into a bowl, add the flours and knead for 5–10 minutes to make a dough. Cover the bowl with a tea towel and leave to rise at room temperature for 45 minutes.

Preheat the oven to 250°C. Put a baking stone, or upside-down baking tray, in the oven to heat.

For step 2, peel the potatoes and cook in salted water until just tender. Drain. Grate finely, spread out on a tray and leave to steam off any excess moisture. Add to the dough along with the flours and ½ tablespoon salt, and knead until smoothly blended.

Roll out the dough very thinly (2mm) and cut out crispbreads using a 10cm round cutter. Place on the baking stone or upside-down baking tray and bake for 1–2 minutes on each side. Remove from the oven and place gently on a wire rack to cool. (You will make about 20 crispbreads; extras can be stored in a well-sealed container at room temperature for 3 months.)

For the sorrel spread, finely chop or blitz the sorrel to a purée. Mix with the onion greens paste.

Quickly fry the sorrel in the clarified butter in a pan over a medium-high heat for about 10 seconds on each side. Drain on kitchen paper and season with salt.

Top the knäckebröd with the radish, garden cress and butter-fried sorrel. Serve the sorrel spread on the side.

Ember-baked leeks, charcoal cream & vendace roe

226

A variation of a signature dish that has been on the menu for a couple of years. We find our guests really enjoy it. It's a great combination: acidity from the charcoal cream, salty fishy vendace roe, umami-rich dried reindeer and crispy potatoes, served with ember-baked leeks.

Serves 4 as a middle course

2 leeks, white part only, about 20cm long
4 tablespoons Charcoal Cream (page 286)
4 tablespoons Crispy Potato (page 282)
1 x 8cm piece Dried Reindeer (page 282)
160g vendace roe (page 289)

Trim off the root of the leeks and rinse in cold water. Place the leeks on top of embers in the wood oven and cook for about 20 minutes, turning the leeks over halfway through, until tender in the centre: check with a skewer or paring knife. Remove from the heat and leave to cool down.

Cut the leeks lengthways through the burnt outer layers (usually 2 or 3). Remove the centre and set the burnt layers aside for later. Cut each leek centre into 10 pieces about 2.5cm long.

To serve, place a spoonful of charcoal cream in the centre of each plate and top with crispy potato. Grate the dried reindeer over to cover. Place 5 pieces of leek around and top each with vendace roe. Garnish with ash from the burnt leek.

Spring lamb & wild garlic

A variety of lamb cuts and cooking techniques – braised breast, grilled rack and seared tenderloin – served with wild garlic capers and leaves. Make the capers from the buds in spring, before the flowers open. The capers can then be enjoyed all year.

Serves 4 as a main course

1 breast of lamb, boned
4 tablespoons Wild Garlic
    Capers (page 281)
300–500ml Lamb Stock or
    Chicken Stock (see
    page 279)
1 teaspoon Apple Cider
    Vinegar (page 280)
1 x 300g rack of lamb
1 x 150g lamb tenderloin
    (fillet)
12 wild garlic leaves
wild garlic flowers, to garnish
sea salt

Preheat the oven to 150°C.

Lay the boned lamb breast flat, fat side down. Season with 1 teaspoon salt and spread over 2 tablespoons of the wild garlic capers. Roll up the lamb and tie with kitchen string into an even bolster shape. Sear all over in a pan over a medium-high heat for 1–2 minutes on each side. Transfer the lamb to a roasting tin. Add enough stock to come halfway up the side of the lamb. Cover with foil and braise in the oven for 1½ hours until tender in the centre: check with a skewer or paring knife. Remove from the oven, lift the lamb on to a board and set aside to rest for 30 minutes.

Boil the braising jus in the tin to reduce by half. Season with the apple cider vinegar and salt to taste.

Grill the rack of lamb over a medium-high heat on the bone side for 4–6 minutes. Turn the rack over and reduce the heat to low. Keep cooking to an internal temperature of 54°C. Remove from the heat and leave to rest for 10 minutes.

Season the tenderloin with salt. Sear in hot embers for 10–15 seconds on each side. Remove from the heat and allow to rest for 5 minutes.

Remove the string from the lamb breast and cut into 4 portions. Glaze in a pan with a spoonful of the reduced lamb braising jus.

Bone the rack and divide both rack and tenderloin into 4 portions. Season the cut surfaces with salt.

Combine the wild garlic leaves and lamb jus in a pan and bring to the boil. Remove from the heat.

Place a piece of lamb breast, rack and tenderloin on each plate. Top with wild garlic leaves and jus and garnish with the remaining capers and flowers.

Grilled redfish, pickled cherry potatoes & truffle seaweed

230

South of Sweden in Skåne are the fields of vegetables and other crops. Many of the fields are full of potatoes and shining, beautiful yellow rapeseed flowers. Rapeseed is of course used for producing oil but the stems are also really tasty. Here they are grilled with redfish. Raw pickled potato adds freshness and a crispy texture.

Serves 4 as a main course

4 x 120g pieces of redfish fillet, skin on
1 tablespoon cooking oil
4 tablespoons Pork Jus (see recipe for Roast Pork, Pickled Kohlrabi, Bread-baked Chanterelle and Kale Cocotte, page 104)
sea salt

For the pickled cherry potatoes
1 tablespoon white wine vinegar
1 tablespoon malt vinegar
3 tablespoons cold-pressed rapeseed oil
200g cherry potatoes (or other small new potatoes)

For the butter-fried rapeseed shoots
12 rapeseed shoots
2 tablespoons Browned Butter (page 285)

For the fried truffle seaweed
4 pieces truffle seaweed (page 289)
500ml cooking oil, for deep-frying

For the pickled potatoes, combine the vinegars, oil and a pinch of salt in a bowl. Whisk to dissolve the salt. Slice the potatoes thinly and rinse in cold water to remove excess starch. Drain on kitchen paper. Add to the bowl and mix with the pickling liquid. Leave to pickle for 30 minutes.

Fry the rapeseed shoots in the browned butter in a pan over a medium-high heat until golden brown.

Deep-fry the seaweed in the oil at 175°C for 5–10 seconds. Drain on kitchen paper.

Season the fish with salt on both sides. Sear on the skin side in the oil in a hot pan for 2–3 minutes – press your hand (or a fish slice) gently over the fish for the first 1–2 minutes to press down the skin and get it evenly fried. Cook almost through, then remove to a tray, placing the fish skin side up. Allow to rest for a minute.

Put a spoonful of pork jus on each plate and place the fish on top. Add the drained pickled potatoes with a spoonful of the pickling liquid, butter-fried rapeseed shoots and fried truffle seaweed.

Turbot on the bone & onion variations

Onions are a favourite ingredient at Ekstedt, and we work with them all around the year. Depending on the season, whether it is fresh picked, or picked really young, or stored and matured over the winter, onions gives a special taste and sweetness in cooking.

Serves 4 as a main course

Knäckebröd with Sorrel
    Spread and Radishes (page
    224), optional, to serve
salt

For the ember-baked
    young onions
2 young onions, unpeeled

For the poached salad onions
2 continental salad onions
30g butter

For the pickled onion
1 tablespoon ättika
    (page 288)
2 tablespoons sugar
1 young onion

For the grilled onion
    greens paste
20 spring onions, green
    part only
2 tablespoons Fish Stock
    (page 278)

For the turbot
4 x 180g portions turbot
    on the bone
2 tablespoons Clarified
    Butter (page 284)

Bury the 2 young onions in the embers of the wood fire and cook for about 30 minutes, turning the onions every 10 minutes, until tender but still firm in the centre: check with a skewer or paring knife. Cool, then remove the outer layer of burnt peel (we keep this to use in other recipes, such as Dairy Beef Fillet in Ash with Caramelised Cream Gravy, page 238). Cut the onions in half lengthways.

Trim the 2 salad onions and cut off the green part (save this for later). Place in a small pan, add the butter and just cover with water. Season with salt. Simmer for about 10 minutes until the onions are tender but still firm in the centre: check with a skewer or paring knife. Remove from the heat and leave to cool down in the poaching liquid.

Heat the ättika and sugar with 3 tablespoons water and ½ teaspoon salt. Pour into a bowl and cool. Peel and thinly slice the onion. Add to the bowl and mix with the pickling liquid. Set aside for at least 30 minutes.

Rinse the spring onion greens in cold water and drain. Grill over high heat embers to mark with grill stripes. Blitz in a blender to a smooth paste. Adjust the consistency with the fish stock. Season with salt.

Preheat the oven to 175°C.

Dry the skin of the turbot on kitchen paper. Season on all sides with salt. Sear on the dark skin side in the clarified butter in a cast-iron pan over a medium-high heat for 2–3 minutes. Flip the fish over and transfer the pan to the oven. Roast for 5–6 minutes until almost cooked all the way to the bone. Remove from the oven and allow to rest for 2 minutes, then brush the skin with the butter in the pan.

Drain the poached salad onions, then cut them in half. Sear on the cut surface in a hot pan. Heat up quickly in the oven together with the ember-baked onions. Gently heat up the onion greens paste until just lukewarm.

Serve the fish with the onion variations and the knäckebröd from page 224, if desired.

Dairy beef fillet in ash with caramelised cream gravy

234

An old retired dairy cow lives the last part of its life in the meadow eating grass and herbs, so its meat is full of flavour. Here it's served with a gravy made from rich cream reduced until caramelised and sweet, and a contrast of tart, acidic semi-dried lingonberries.

Serves 4 as a middle course

For the semi-dried lingonberries
4 tablespoons lingonberries (page 288), fresh or frozen

For the caramelised cream gravy
400ml double cream
1 tablespoon Beef Demiglace (page 280)
sea salt

For the dairy beef fillet
3 tablespoons burnt skin from ember-baked onion or leeks (see recipe for Turbot on the Bone and Onion Variations, page 232)
1 x 400g dairy beef/Basque beef fillet (page 288)
1 tablespoon Clarified Butter (page 284)
sea salt

Preheat the oven to 80°C.

Spread out the lingonberries on a tray and dry in the oven for about 2 hours until the skin is dried and the berries shrink by half, but are still a bit juicy inside. (This could also be done at a lower temperature but the drying time would be longer.)

To make the gravy, pour the cream into a wide pan and reduce over a medium-high heat until thick and very light brown with a caramelised aroma. Remove from the heat and stir in the beef demiglace. Season with salt.

Preheat the oven to 150°C.

Finely chop the burnt onion skin, until it resembles ash, and season with a pinch of salt.

Season the beef with salt, then sear on all sides in the clarified butter in a hot pan – about 20 seconds per side. Place the fillet on a rack in a roasting tin and roast to an internal temperature of 50°C. Remove from the oven and leave to rest for 10 minutes. Reheat the pan used for searing. Dry the fillet with kitchen paper and sear quickly on all sides in the hot pan.

Slice the fillet into 4 portions. Roll the edges in the onion ash. Place a spoonful of gravy in the centre of each plate. Place the beef on the gravy and top with semi-dried lingonberries.

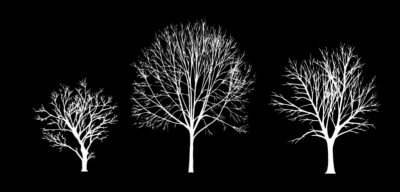

Hay-flamed

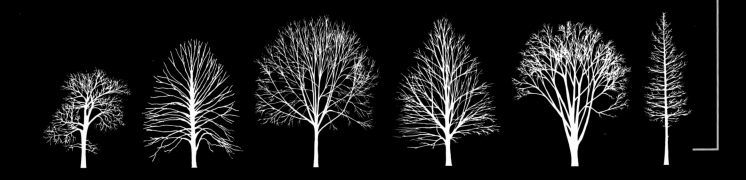

Hay-flamed salad & smoked butter

Mixed salad is served at most restaurants all over the world. I think this is the obvious way to prepare it at Ekstedt, with the leaves seasoned with smoked butter and just touching the flames from the open fire.

Serves 4 as a middle course

12–20 leaves of spring salad (frisée, escarole, radicchio, romaine)
2 tablespoons Smoked Butter (page 285), melted
a bunch of hay
1 teaspoon Hay Ash (page 283)

For the crispy dried leek roots
2 leeks with 5–6cm roots
sea salt

Preheat the oven to 75°C. Cut the roots from the leeks (keep the leeks for another recipe). Rinse in cold water and drain. Place on a silicone mat on a baking tray and dry in the oven for about 2 hours until crispy. (Leave the oven door slightly ajar to avoid humidity.) Season the dried roots with salt.

Pick the salad leaves and rinse in cold water. Drain or spin dry.

Brush the salad leaves with the melted smoked butter. Place in a metal sieve and sear lightly over embers with burning hay.

Top with the dried leek roots and hay ash.

Wild asparagus, soured cream & preserved lemon confit

240

One of my favourite ingredients that I discovered when abroad is preserved lemon. It gives a wonderful aroma and a deep rich, fresh lemon flavour. We buy the lemons ready-made since we do not have lemon farmers in Scandinavia and so cannot get hold of the best lemons. If you can, it is quite easy to preserve your own lemons in salt, although you'll have to wait a month before enjoying them.

Serves 4 as a snack

16–25 wild asparagus spears
a bunch of hay
1 tablespoon melted butter
2 tablespoons soured cream
a bunch of garden cress
sea salt

For the preserved lemon confit
4 quarters preserved lemon
   (page 289)

Remove the pips from the lemon quarters. Blitz the lemons in a blender to a smooth purée. Add a little water if needed.

Place the asparagus in a metal sieve and sear lightly over embers for 20 seconds. Pile the hay on the embers, underneath the sieve of asparagus. Once the hay is alight, let it burn out. Remove the asparagus from the heat and brush off the ash. Brush the spears with the melted butter and season with salt.

Serve the asparagus with the lemon confit, soured cream and garden cress.

Semi-raw hay-flamed seas bass, sorrel & Swedish ponzu

242

A truly Japanese-inspired dish adapted to a Swedish context, using local ingredients – our version of ponzu is made from the salty rich jus of fermented celery filled with umami aroma, home-made apple cider vinegar and tar syrup.

Serves 4 as a middle course

1 x 180g piece of sea bass
    fillet, skin on
1 tablespoon sea salt
a bunch of hay
12 red sorrel leaves
12 borage flowers

For the Swedish ponzu
2 tablespoons juice from
    Fermented Celery
    (page 281)
1 tablespoon Apple Cider
    Vinegar (page 280)
50ml tar syrup (page 289)

Remove the scales from the fish. Combine 200ml water with the sea salt in a bowl and whisk to dissolve the salt. Add the fish and set aside to brine for 20 minutes. Remove the fish from the brine and dry with kitchen paper.

Combine the ingredients for the Swedish ponzu. Set aside.

Place the fish, skin side down, on a cold grill rack about 20cm over the fire (no embers). Place the hay under the fish and once alight let it burn to ash.

Cut the fillet into 4 portions and slice each portion into 3 pieces. Top with Swedish ponzu and the sorrel and borage flowers.

Beef, black garlic, sorrel, salsify & sunflower seeds

With this cooking technique, very thin slices of beef sirloin are threaded on to skewers, which will make the surface uneven, and then cooked at a really hot temperature for a short time. From raw through the Maillard reaction to a crispy grilled result. I find it so tasty!

Serves 4 as a middle course

4 x 40g pieces of boneless beef
sirloin, sliced 5mm thick
a bunch of hay
3 tablespoons Black Garlic
Emulsion (page 281)
12 slices Fermented Salsify
plus 1 tablespoon juice
(see recipe for Butternut
Squash, Fermented Salsify
and Vegetable Foam,
page 130)
12–16 fresh sorrel leaves

For the flamed salsify
2–3 salsify
Browned Butter (page 285)

For the sorrel oil
a bunch of sorrel
2 tablespoons sea salt
½ tablespoon baking powder
100ml rapeseed oil

*For the roasted
  sunflower seeds*
1 tablespoon dry-aged beef
fat or tallow
2 tablespoons sunflower
seeds

Using a meat mallet, pound the slices of beef to flatten them and break down the fibres. Put each piece of meat on 2 skewers, keeping the slices flat.

For the flamed salsify, peel the salsify and rinse in cold water. Grill on a rack over medium-high embers until tender but still firm in the middle: check with a skewer or paring knife. Cool down, then peel off the burnt surface (easiest done with your hands). Cut into 4–5cm pieces; you need 12 pieces. Before serving, fry in the browned butter on a medium-low heat for 2–3 minutes.

For the sorrel oil, pick the sorrel leaves and rinse in cold water. Add the salt to 500ml water in a pan and bring to the boil in a pan. Add the baking powder and stir. Add the sorrel and blanch for 10 seconds. Drain and cool down in cold water. Drain again and squeeze out any excess water. Blitz the sorrel with the oil in a blender. Strain through a muslin-lined sieve. (Use fresh, or store in the freezer to use for a salad dressing.)

Heat a pan over a medium-high heat. Add the beef fat and sunflower seeds. Sauté for 2–3 minutes until golden brown. Drain on kitchen paper, reserving the beef fat.

Mix 1 tablespoon of the sorrel oil with the fermented salsify juice.

Place the beef 5–7cm above high heat embers and grill for 10 seconds on one side only. Pile a bunch of hay on top of the embers and place the beef on top of that. Once the hay is alight, let it burn out for 5–10 seconds. Remove the beef from the heat.

Serve the beef on a spoonful of black garlic emulsion, with the butter-fried flamed salsify, fermented salsify, sorrel oil mixed with fermentation juice, sunflower seeds and fresh sorrel leaves brushed with beef fat.

Mackerel belly with roasted pickled mustard seeds & raw leeks

Using the belly of the fish adds an extra fatty texture that goes very well with the slightly spicy, sweet and sour mustard seeds and crispy, slightly bitter, raw young leek.

Serves 4 as a main course

4 x 80g pieces of mackerel belly (the fattest middle part of the fillet), skin on
a bunch of hay
sea salt

For the roasted pickled yellow mustard seeds
1½ tablespoons yellow mustard seeds
50ml ättika (page 288)
100g sugar

For the raw leeks
2–3 young leeks, white part only

Roast the mustard seeds in a pan over a medium heat until golden brown, stirring constantly. Remove from the pan. Combine the ättika, sugar, 150ml water and 1 teaspoon salt in a saucepan and bring to the boil. Add the roasted mustard seeds and simmer for 20 minutes. Remove from the heat and set aside to cool. Drain the seeds for serving.

Clean the leeks in cold running water. Cut in half lengthways, then slice thinly into shreds. Add ½ teaspoon salt and knead to a soft texture.

Season the mackerel with 1 tablespoon salt, then leave for 20 minutes.

Rinse the fish in cold water. Drain and dry with kitchen paper. Sear on the skin side in a cast-iron pan over a high heat for 20–30 seconds. Remove from the pan and place on a grill rack over medium-high heat embers. Pile the hay on top of the fish, set alight and let it burn for 5–10 seconds.

Serve the fish with the kneaded leeks and pickled roasted mustard seeds plus a teaspoon of their brine.

Hay-flamed sweetbread, aigre-doux & blackened young garlic

248

Inspired by the French sweet and sour sauce aigre-doux, with tar syrup to add Nordic flavours. The sauce is served warm with delicate young garlic and hay-flamed veal sweetbreads.

Serves 4 as a middle course

4 x 50g pieces of veal
  sweetbreads
1 x 5cm piece continental
  salad onion (white part
  only)
a bunch of hay

For the aigre-doux
2 tablespoons malt vinegar
2 tablespoons brown sugar
2 tablespoons Chicken Stock
  (page 279)
1 tablespoon tar syrup
  (page 289)

*For the blackened young
  garlic*
2 young garlic stems (bulb
  and green leaves)
1 tablespoon Smoked Butter
  (page 285)

Blanch the sweetbreads in boiling water for 30 seconds. Remove from the water and cool, then trim off all sinew and gristle.

For the aigre-doux, combine the vinegar, brown sugar, chicken stock and tar syrup in a saucepan. Bring to the boil and simmer to reduce to about 2 tablespoons.

Cut the garlic in half lengthways. Sear on the cut surfaces in a hot cast-iron pan for about 45 seconds. Remove from the heat and brush with the smoked butter.

Slice the salad onion very thinly lengthways into shreds and drop into iced water to crisp.

Season the sweetbread pieces and grill on a rack over medium-high heat embers for 20 seconds on each side. Place a bunch of hay on top of the embers, under the rack of sweetbreads. Once the hay is alight, let it burn for 5–10 seconds to ash. Remove the sweetbreads from the heat and brush off the ash.

Serve the sweetbreads with the warm aigre-doux, blackened young garlic and crisp salad onion shreds.

Open Fire

Arctic king crab with blackcurrant wood

252

This dish is a perfect example of a great product meeting the fires of the Ekstedt kitchen. In the 1960s king crab from the Pacific Ocean around Alaska and Japan were introduced to the Barents Sea and today these large crustaceans are spreading strongly south along the Norwegian coast.

Serves 4 as a middle course

4 raw king crab legs in their shells, about 12cm long
2 tablespoons melted Smoked Butter (page 285)
2–3 branches of blackcurrant wood
1 teaspoon Hay Salt (page 283)

Place the crab legs on the embers and cook for 2–3 minutes on each side. Remove from the heat. With sharp kitchen scissors, cut open the shell on both sides and carefully loosen the crab meat from the shell (save one half of each shell). Remove the 2 cartilage bones inside the crab meat, then place the piece of meat back in the shell. Brush with melted smoked butter.

Set a grill rack above the fire. Place the crab, shell side down, on the rack and add branches of blackcurrant wood to the embers. Allow to flame and smoke for 2 minutes.

Remove the crab legs from the heat and season with the hay salt.

Pan-seared razor clams with lovage & smoked butter

254

These beautiful molluscs are getting more and more popular in Scandinavia, picked on the beaches along the Atlantic coast of Denmark and Sweden. Be very careful not to overcook the clams. They just need a really quick heating to be perfectly cooked, juicy and tender.

Serves 4 as a middle course

12 razor clams
2 tablespoons Smoked Butter
   (page 285)
1 tablespoon chopped chives

Rinse the clams under cold running water for 10 minutes. Place in a bowl with 3 litres cold water and leave in the fridge for 24 hours to purge the sand from the shells. Rinse the clams under cold running water again for 10 minutes. Drain in a colander for 10 minutes.

For the lovage purée
200ml roughly chopped
   lovage
½ garlic clove, peeled

Blanch the lovage in boiling water for 10 seconds. Drain and cool down in iced water. Squeeze out any excess water and blitz in a blender to a smooth purée; add a tiny bit of water if needed. Grate the garlic and season the purée with it. (It is difficult to make a smaller quantity of this; leftover purée can be kept in the fridge for 3 days.)

Heat up a wide cast-iron pan to smoking hot over the fire. Add the clams, remove from the heat and sear for 1 minute. Add the smoked butter and, as it melts and foams, swirl to mix with the clam juices. Remove the clams and reduce the jus in the pan by about half over a medium-high heat.

Remove one side of each clam shell and place the clams on the plates. Drizzle the jus from the pan on top, along with the lovage purée and chopped chives.

Seafood salad platter

256

We are privileged to have amazing seafood and shellfish from our west coast in the northern Atlantic Ocean. Because of the cold water, lobsters, langoustines, mussels, squid and oysters grow slowly, which I believe has a positive effect, especially for shellfish.

Serves 4 as a snack

1 x 200g piece of
    prepared squid
1 tablespoon sugar
1 tablespoon sea salt
4 langoustines
2 sprigs of thyme
½ garlic clove, peeled
30g butter
200ml seaweed salad
    (page 289)
½ lemon

Using a sharp knife, score shallow diagonal cuts in a criss-cross pattern on the surface of the piece of squid, taking care not to cut right through. Combine the sugar and salt with 200ml water in a bowl and whisk to dissolve. Add the squid and set aside to brine for 20 minutes at room temperature.

Pull the heads off the langoustines. Scrape out the butter/brain in the heads and set aside. Pull off the claws. Crush the heads and claws and sauté with the thyme and garlic in the butter over a medium-high heat for 5 minutes. Remove from the heat and infuse for 10 minutes. Strain the resulting langoustine butter and set aside.

Sear the langoustines in a hot cast-iron pan over the open fire, curved upper side first, pressing down with your hand to prevent them curling. Sear for about 1 minute on each side. Remove from the heat and leave to rest for 2 minutes. Cut the langoustines in half lengthways and remove the intestinal tract. Brush the langoustines with the langoustine butter.

Grill the squid on a rack over high heat embers – start with 2–3 minutes on the scored side to give colour, then turn over and grill for a further 1 minute. Cut the squid into 4 portions.

Toss the seaweed salad with the langoustine butter/brain, remaining langoustine butter and freshly squeezed lemon juice. Serve with the squid and langoustines.

Wild duck breast, Jerusalem artichoke, truffle & grilled chard

258

Hunting season for wild duck is late autumn. A common game bird all over Sweden, except in the very north, it is usually hunted using a shotgun loaded with multiple metallic shot. That is why it's important to try to remove all shot when serving. Like other game, wild duck meat is quite lean, so take care when searing and make sure to give it a good rest before serving.

Serves 4 as a main course

For the seared wild
duck breasts
1 wild duck breast crown
(on the bone)
1 tablespoon rapeseed oil

For the seared Jerusalem
artichokes
200g Jerusalem artichokes,
peeled and cut into
5mm dice
30g Clarified Butter
(page 284)

For the grilled chard
8 Swiss chard leaves
1 tablespoon Smoked Butter
(page 285)

For the black truffle duck jus
100ml Wild Duck Jus
(page 70)
Apple Cider Vinegar
(page 280) to taste
20g black winter truffle,
finely chopped
sea salt

Sear the duck breast crown in the oil in a cast-iron pan over the open fire to an internal temperature of 45°C and to give the skin a nice golden colour. Remove the breast crown from the pan and leave to rest for half the time it has been cooking.

Meanwhile, pan-fry the artichokes in the clarified butter in a cast-iron pan until just tender but still firm in the centre.

Brush the chard with smoked butter, then grill on embers.

For the black truffle duck jus, reduce the duck jus to 4 tablespoons and season with apple cider vinegar and salt.

To serve, carve out the 2 breasts from the bone and flash in the oven to heat. Trim off the edges and cut each breast in half lengthways. Add the black truffle to the duck jus. Serve the duck with the grilled chard, Jerusalem artichokes and jus.

Pickled mackerel loin, cold-pressed rapeseed oil & edible flowers

260

Flowers are not only beautiful in the garden, but also great in a plate of food. Many of our most common garden flowers are edible, but we also pick wildflowers in the forests around Stockholm. (Never eat flowers that you are not sure about because some are poisonous. Also, do not pick plants near the roadside as they will have been contaminated with exhaust gases, emissions and pesticides. As a rule of thumb, pick at least 50 metres from the roadside.)

Serves 4 as a middle course

1 mackerel, filleted (about 240g fillets)
½ tablespoon sea salt
100ml Apple Cider Vinegar (page 280)
a bunch of edible flowers and leaves (dill, sweet cecily, wild garlic flowers, chive flowers)

For the vinegar dressing
2 tablespoons Apple Cider Vinegar (page 280)
2 tablespoons cold-pressed rapeseed oil

Lay each mackerel fillet on a chopping board, skin side up. At one of the corners of the thick end of the fillet, tease away the top membrane/very thin skin using your finger. Once you've got enough to pinch between your fingers, peel down gently towards the tail. Repeat with the other fillet. Turn the fillets over and, using a sharp knife, cut vertically down each fillet, a couple of millimetres either side of the central line of smaller pinbones, creating 4 bone-free fillet loins. Cut these in half, to make 2 pieces per portion.

Combine 500ml water and the salt, whisking to dissolve the salt. Cover the fish loins with the liquid and leave to brine for 20 minutes. Remove the mackerel loins from the brine and rinse in cold water. Cover with the apple cider vinegar and set aside for 20 minutes.

Combine the vinegar and rapeseed oil for the dressing.

Place the mackerel loins in bowls, drizzle over the dressing and garnish with the leaves and flowers.

Flambadou

Radishes with home-made butter & hay salt

Flambadou

Spring / Summer

266

One of my favourite childhood memories is eating freshly harvested raw radish and cooked sweet red beetroots with a piece of cold butter. When you grow up your tastes change and mature – but I still love radishes, and in this recipe we added some fatty and smoky aromas to them with the flambadou and by seasoning butter with hay salt.

Serves 4 as a snack

8–10 large radishes
  (with leaves)
1 x 15g piece of beef fat or
  tallow from dry-aged beef
  (page 288)
1 daisy flower
4 tablespoons Home-made
  Butter (page 284)
1 teaspoon Hay Salt
  (page 283)

Clean and trim the radishes (keep the green leaves). Cut into quarters and drain on kitchen paper.

Place the radish quarters, cut surface up, on an untreated wooden plank. Sear each radish for 5 seconds with burning beef fat from the flambadou.

Garnish with radish leaves and daisy flower petals. Serve the butter on the side topped with hay salt.

Flambadou white asparagus & apple

268

White asparagus has a short season and there is always a period of craving it in early spring before it arrives. But it is worth waiting for. Poaching this delicate vegetable in whey gives it an acidity that is balanced by searing it in beef fat from the flambadou.

Serves 4 as a snack

2 large white asparagus
    spears
200ml whey (page 289)
juice of ½ lemon
½ teaspoon sea salt
1 tart apple
2 tablespoons Apple Cider
    Vinegar (page 280)
1 x 15g piece of beef fat or
    tallow from dry-aged beef
    (page 288)
Herb Oil (page 283)

Peel each asparagus stalk and cut off the tough base. Cut each spear in half lengthways.

Combine the whey, lemon juice and salt in a saucepan and poach the asparagus until tender but still a bit firm in the middle. Remove from the whey and drain on kitchen paper.

Peel the apple and cut into fine dice. Combine with the vinegar.

Place the asparagus, cut side up, on an untreated wooden plank. Sear each spear for 5 seconds with burning beef fat from the flambadou.

Top each asparagus half with diced apple plus ½ teaspoon of the vinegar used for the apple. Add a drizzle of herb oil.

Purple romanesco & hill mustard flower

Flambadou

Spring / Summer

270

Romanesco is a cross between cauliflower and broccoli. Here it is sautéed in butter and then seared with the flambadou. It's served topped with tasty, slightly spicy hill mustard flowers.

Serves 4 as a snack

4 florets of purple or green
    romanesco, each 3 x 3cm
15g butter
1 x 15g piece of beef fat or
    tallow from dry-aged beef
    (page 288)
8 hill mustard flowers
½ teaspoon burnt skin
    from ember-baked onion
    or leeks (see recipe for
    Onion Confit Purée and
    Brussels Sprouts, page 102,
    or Ember-baked Leeks,
    Charcoal Cream and
    Vendace Roe, page 226)

Sauté the romanesco in the butter in a pan over a medium-high heat for 3–5 minutes until golden brown.

Place the romanesco, cut surface up, on an untreated wooden plank. Sear the romanesco for 6–8 seconds with burning beef fat from the flambadou.

Top with the hill mustard flowers and garnish with the onion/leek ash.

Pork filet mignon, charcoal syrup & hay salt

272

The beautiful pork inner fillet is a tender and tasty piece of meat when treated right. We precook it to the perfect temperature, let it rest and then sear with the flambadou.

Serves 4 as a snack

1 x 200g piece of pork tenderloin (fillet)

1 x 15g piece of beef fat or tallow from dry-aged beef (page 288)

2 teaspoons Hay Salt (page 283)

sea salt

For the charcoal syrup

1 tablespoon tar syrup (page 289)

3 tablespoons meadowsweet syrup (page 289)

Trim the pork and season with salt. Place on a rack over the fire at medium-high heat (100–120°C). Roast to an internal temperature of 58°C, which will take 40–60 minutes. During cooking, turn the pork every 10–15 minutes.

Mix together the tar and meadowsweet syrups.

Place the pork on an untreated wooden plank. Sear with burning beef fat from the flambadou for about 15 seconds.

Cut the pork into 8 slices. Brush with the syrup and season with hay salt.

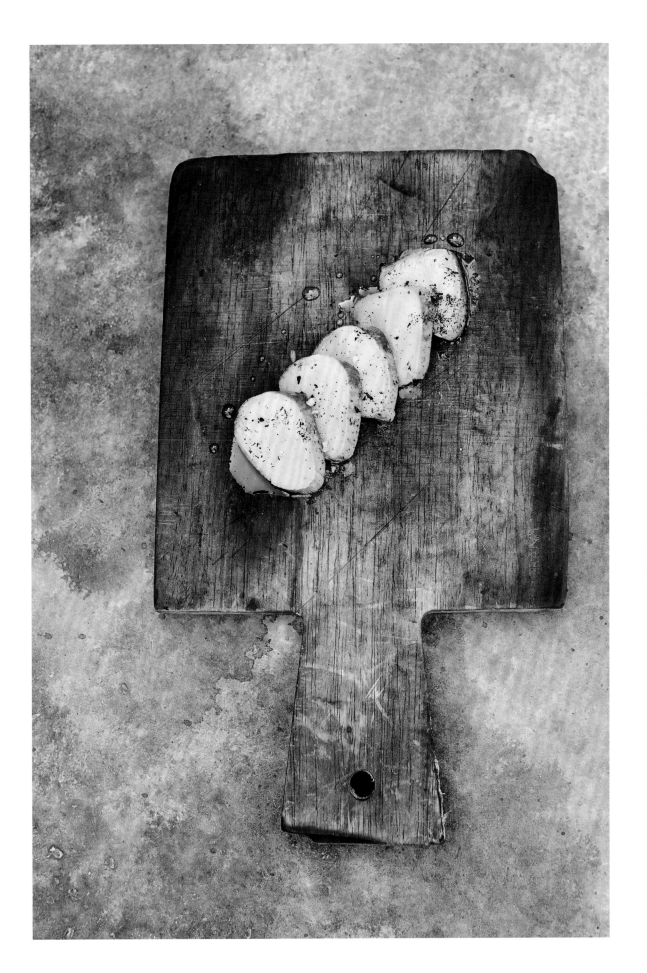

Sweet shrimps with smoked mayonnaise

Flambadou
Spring / Summer

274

Simple yet sublime: shrimps seared in burning beef fat, served with a smoky mayonnaise. Enjoy!

Serves 4 as a snack

12 sweet shrimps or prawns
1 garlic clove
2 shallots
½ carrot
1 bay leaf
1 sprig of thyme
3 black peppercorns
15g butter
150ml rapeseed oil
½ tablespoon Swedish
   mustard (page 289)
½ tablespoon ättika
   (page 288)
1 egg yolk
1 x 15g piece of beef fat or
   tallow from dry-aged beef
   (page 288)
sea salt

Peel the shrimps, leaving on the ends of the tails. Save all the shells.

Peel and chop the garlic, shallots and carrot. Sauté the shrimp shells and vegetables with the bay leaf, thyme and peppercorns in the butter in a pan over a medium-high heat for about 3 minutes, without colouring. Remove from the heat.

Add the rapeseed oil and hot smoke for 20 minutes. Remove from the smoker and cool down, then strain the smoked oil through a sieve.

Combine the mustard and ättika with the egg yolk in a bowl. Add the smoked oil drop by drop, whisking constantly to emulsify. Season with salt.

Place the shrimps tight together on an untreated wooden plank. Sear for 8–10 seconds with burning beef fat from the flambadou.

Serve the shrimps warm with the smoked mayonnaise for dipping.

The End

Vegetable stock

Fish stock

Makes 1.8 litres

Makes 1 litre

2 white onions,
    cut in half
1 carrot
½ celery stick
3 garlic cloves,
    peeled
2 bay leaves
2 sprigs of parsley
3 sprigs of thyme

Place the onion halves, cut side down, on top of a wood cooking stove, or in a cast-iron pan, and roast until browned or charred. Meanwhile, cut the carrot and celery roughly into 3cm cubes.

Put all the ingredients into a large pan with 2 litres water. Bring to the boil and simmer for 20 minutes. Remove from the heat and leave to sit for an hour.

Strain the stock but do not pour through the last of the stock in the bottom of the pan. Use fresh or store in the fridge for 3 days.

1kg turbot bones
3 yellow onions
2 carrots
1 celery stick
2 bay leaves
5 sprigs of thyme
6 black
    peppercorns

Preheat the oven to 175°C. Roast the turbot bones for about 30 minutes until golden brown.

Peel the onions and carrots, and cut all the vegetables into roughly 3 x 3cm pieces.

Combine the turbot bones, vegetables and flavourings in a wide pot and add 1.3 litres water. Bring to the boil and simmer for 20 minutes. Remove from the heat and leave to settle for 30 minutes.

Strain through a sieve into a clean pan. Bring to the boil and reduce to 1 litre. The stock can be kept in the fridge for 3–5 days.

Chicken stock

Lamb stock

Makes 1 litre

Makes 1 litre

1kg raw chicken
  bones
about 2
  tablespoons
  Clarified Butter
  (page 284), plus
  extra to drizzle
1 large carrot,
  roughly
  chopped
1 onion, roughly
  chopped
2 celery sticks,
  roughly
  chopped
1 leek, sliced
1 bay leaf
3 sprigs of thyme
3 garlic cloves,
  peeled
sea salt and
  freshly ground
  black pepper

Preheat the oven to 175°C.
Spread out the bones in a
large roasting tin and drizzle
over a little clarified butter
to coat. Roast for 30–45
minutes, turning the
bones over halfway, until
evenly browned.

Heat the 2 tablespoons
clarified butter in a large
stockpot and add the
vegetables, herbs and garlic.
Sauté over a medium heat,
stirring occasionally, until
the vegetables are golden.
Add the chicken bones, then
pour in enough cold water to
cover, about 1.5 litres. Season
lightly with salt and pepper.
Bring to the boil, skimming
off any scum that rises to the
surface. Reduce the heat and
simmer gently for 1 hour.

Leave the stock to stand for
a few minutes to cool slightly
and allow the ingredients
to settle before straining
through a fine sieve.

Use fresh stock within
5 days or keep frozen for
up to 3 months.

500g lamb bones
2 tablespoons
  Clarified Butter
  (page 284), plus
  extra to drizzle
1 large yellow
  onion, roughly
  chopped
2 carrots, roughly
  chopped
1 celery stick,
  roughly
  chopped
6 garlic cloves,
  peeled
1 teaspoon black
  peppercorns
1 bay leaf
a few sprigs of
  thyme and flat-
  leaf parsley

Preheat the oven to 175°C.
Spread out the bones in a
large roasting tin and drizzle
over a little clarified butter
to coat. Roast for 45–60
minutes, turning the
bones over halfway, until
evenly browned.

Heat the 2 tablespoons
clarified butter in a large
stockpot and add the
vegetables and garlic. Sauté,
stirring occasionally, over
a medium-high heat until
golden brown. Add the bones
to the stockpot and pour in
enough water to cover, about
1.5 litres. Bring to a simmer
and skim off the froth and
scum that rises to the surface.

Add the peppercorns and
herbs. Simmer the stock for
4 hours, then take the pan off
the heat. Allow to stand for a
few minutes before straining
the stock through a fine
sieve. Cool the stock to room
temperature, then cover and
chill for up to 48 hours. The
fat from the stock will rise
and congeal on the surface
and can then be removed
with a spoon and discarded.

Fresh stock should be used
within 5 days or keep frozen
for up to 3 months.

Beef demiglace

Apple cider vinegar

Makes 400ml

2 tablespoons
   Clarified Butter
   (page 284)
1 onion, chopped
1 carrot, chopped
½ head celeriac,
   chopped
2 tablespoons
   plain flour
800ml beef stock
1 bay leaf
3 sprigs of thyme
6 sprigs of parsley
8 black
   peppercorns

Heat the clarified butter in a heavy-bottomed pan over a medium heat. Add the onion, carrot and celeriac, and sauté them for a couple of minutes. Sprinkle in the flour and stir, then cook, stirring frequently, for about 3 minutes until the flour is lightly browned, but not burnt.

Whisk in the beef stock and bring to the boil. Add the herbs and peppercorns. Leave to simmer for about 1 hour until reduced by half to a thick sauce consistency.

Strain through a fine sieve or a sieve lined with muslin. Demiglace can be kept in the fridge for 2 weeks or a couple of months frozen.

When making your own apple cider vinegar, wash all the containers you are going to use with hot, soapy water. More importantly, scrub your hands and nails clean before beginning the process.

**Makes about
   1 litre**

10 organic apples
3 tablespoons
   brown sugar

Wash the apples in running water. Cut them into quarters and place in a large clean jar.

Mix the sugar with 300ml water, whisking to dissolve. Pour over the apples. Add enough extra water to the jar so that the apples are covered. Cover the jar with a piece of muslin, but don't secure it tightly: the cloth should just rest lightly on the top so that the mixture gets more oxygen. Store this covered jar in a warm, dark place for about 6 months. Stir once a week.

After the 6-month fermentation period, you will find a layer of scum has formed on top of the liquid. This is due to normal bacteria and is formed as alcohol turns into vinegar.

Take another large, clean, wide-mouthed glass jar and filter the liquid through the muslin into it. Use the same piece of muslin to cover the new jar of liquid. Leave the jar in a warm, dark place for a further 5–6 weeks.

Transfer the vinegar into smaller jars. Cover and store in the fridge.

Black garlic emulsion

Makes about 200g

1 egg
3 tablespoons chopped black garlic (page 288)
150g Browned Butter (page 285)
sea salt

Cook the egg in boiling water for 2 minutes, then drain and cool down. Crack the egg and scoop it out into a blender. Add the black garlic and blitz on a high speed to a smooth purée.

Heat the browned butter to about 60°C. Gradually add the butter to the garlic mixture, mixing constantly, to emulsify. Season with salt.

The emulsion can be kept in the fridge for 3 days. Return to room temperature for serving.

Sunflower seed emulsion

Makes 300g

100g sunflower seeds
130ml rapeseed oil
50ml soy sauce
50ml white wine vinegar

Roast the sunflower seeds in 30ml of the oil in a frying pan over a medium heat until golden brown. Leave to cool.

Put the sunflower seeds, soy sauce and vinegar into a blender or small food processor and blitz to a smooth paste. With the motor running, gradually add the remaining rapeseed oil to emulsify.

The emulsion can be kept in the fridge for 5 days.

Fermented celery

Makes 500g

500g celery
10g sea salt

Trim off the root from the celery and rinse in cold water. Combine with the salt and vacuum pack. Leave to ferment at room temperature for 2 weeks, then store in the fridge where it will keep for months.

Wild garlic capers

Makes 200g

200g wild garlic (ramsons) buds
150ml ättika (page 288)
150g caster sugar
60g sea salt

Clean the garlic buds in cold running water. Combine the ättika, sugar, salt and 300ml water in a bowl, whisking to dissolve the sugar and salt.

Immerse the buds in the liquid and leave to brine in the fridge for 4 days before using. The capers can be kept, in brine, in the fridge for a year (when it will be time to make a new season's batch).

Crispy potato

Dried reindeer

Makes 30–50g

Makes 50g

500g potatoes
(use a starchy,
rich variety
such as Andean
Sunrise)
cooking oil, for
deep-frying
sea salt

Peel the potatoes and grate
on the fine holes of a regular
grater. Rinse in running cold
water until all the starch
is gone. Drain in a sieve
and press out excess water
by hand.

Heat the oil in a deep, wide
pan to 180°C. Split the
potatoes into 3–5 batches
and fry one batch at a time.
Add to the hot oil and stir
with a whisk during the
first 10–20 seconds to avoid
lumps. Fry the potatoes to
a golden brown. Drain on
kitchen paper and season
with salt.

The potatoes can be stored
in a dry place at room
temperature for 1 week.

120g sea salt
300g boned
reindeer meat
from the inner
thigh (haunch)

Combine the salt with 1 litre
water in a bowl, whisking to
dissolve the salt.

Trim the meat to remove
all fat and sinew and cut
lengthways into pieces
5–7cm in diameter. Immerse
in the salted water and leave
in the fridge to brine for 24
hours.

Drain the meat and rinse in
cold running water. Place on
a meat hook and hang above
the fire at around 30°C to
cold smoke for 3 hours.

Leave to hang on a meat
hook in a dry place,
uncovered, for 10 days at
room temperature to dry
out. Store in a container
in the fridge.

Smoked oil

Makes 200ml

200ml rapeseed
oil
a branch of
juniper, a birch
log or smoking
chips

Light up a smoker with your
choice of fuel – no warmer
than 100°C. Put the oil in
a heat-resistant pan or jug
and place in the smoker.
Leave to smoke for about
30 minutes, then taste to see
if it needs longer for more
smoky flavour.

Use fresh or store in the
fridge for up to 2 weeks.

Herb oil

Makes 100ml

300ml rapeseed
oil
a bunch of
hard herbs,
e.g. thyme,
rosemary,
lavender (about
50g), roughly
chopped
a bunch of
spinach
(200–300ml)
a bunch of soft
herbs, e.g.
lovage, wild
garlic leaves,
oregano,
sage (about
100g), roughly
chopped

Combine 150ml oil and the
hard herbs in a pan and heat
up to 70°C for 20 minutes.

Strain out the hard herbs and
pour the oil into a blender.
Add the spinach and soft
herbs and blitz for a minute.
Add the remaining 150ml
oil and keep blitzing for a
minute. Strain through a
coffee filter.

The oil can be kept for 3
days in the fridge. (If you are
aiming for an oil flavoured
with a single seasonal herb,
just use that herb plus
spinach.)

Hay ash

**Makes 3
tablespoons**

a bunch of hay

Place the hay in a fire-
resistant tray or cast-iron pan
and set alight. Make sure all
the hay is burnt. Grind the
ash in a mortar and press
through a sieve.

Stored covered and dry, the
ash will keep for 1 month.

Hay salt

**Makes about 2
tablespoons**

about 100g hay
3 tablespoons sea
salt

Place the hay in a fire-
resistant tray or cast-iron
pan and set it alight. Make
sure all the hay is burned
down to ashes. Combine the
salt and ashes in a mortar
and grind to a powder.
Sift through a sieve.

Store covered in a dry
place where it will keep
for 1 month.

Home-made butter

Clarified butter

At the restaurant we always make our own butter, using the previous batch of butter for sourness. The squeezed-out buttermilk can be used for bread baking or making your own soured cream.

Makes 300g

3 litres whipping cream
300g soured cream (or leftover butter from previous batch)
sea salt

Combine the cream and soured cream in a bowl and mix together gently until smooth. Cover and leave at room temperature for about 24 hours. The mix should taste slightly sour.

Chill to about 10°C, then use an electric mixer to whisk on medium speed until the liquid has separated – you will see light yellow lumps in the liquid (this is buttermilk).

Squeeze the buttermilk out of the lumps with very clean hands. Work the butter as long as you want – the more it is squeezed and the more buttermilk that is removed, the richer and longer-lasting the butter will be. But at the same time you will lose some of the butter's acidity and pleasant aroma. I prefer not to over-work it. However, if I want a butter that can be kept for up to 1 month, I'll squeeze out as much buttermilk as possible, then add some cold water and continue to work the butter until all the water has been squeezed out.

Season the butter with salt if desired. Store, covered, in the fridge.

Makes 160g

200g unsalted butter

Put the butter in a saucepan and melt over a medium-high heat. Once the butter is fully melted, allow it to continue to heat until it comes to a gentle boil. The milk proteins will first form a thin white layer over the entire surface, then expand into a thicker foam.

Eventually, as the butter boils, the foam coating will break apart into smaller clusters. The foam will ultimately sink to the bottom of the pan as the butter continues bubbling away. You'll know that it's nearly done when the bubbling activity calms and then mostly ceases – evidence that the water has all evaporated.

Pour the clear butter through a muslin-lined sieve or a coffee filter to remove the browned bits, leaving the residue of the milky foam in the pan. Store the clarified butter in the fridge where it will keep for months.

Smoked butter

Browned butter

Makes 200g

Makes 80g

200g unsalted
butter
a branch of
juniper, a birch
log or smoking
chips

Temper the butter to room
temperature. Light up a
smoker with your choice
of fuel – no warmer than
100°C. Place the butter in
a heat-resistant pan or jug
and place in the smoker.
Leave to smoke for about
30 minutes, then taste the
butter to see if it needs longer
for more smoky flavour. It
will probably be melted and
separated as butter melts
around 40°C.

Cool down to around room
temperature, then stir to mix
the separated butter again
and make it creamy. Use
fresh or keep in the fridge
for up to 2 weeks.

100g unsalted
butter
a pinch of sea
salt (1.2g: 1.5%
of the butter
weight)

Melt the butter in a saucepan
over a medium heat. Increase
the heat. When the butter
begins to simmer, start
stirring with a whisk – this
will prevent particles from
settling on the bottom and
getting burnt. Keep stirring
until the butter is lightly
browned. Do not let it burn.

Pour the butter into a bowl
and season with the salt. Use
fresh or store in a screwtop
jar, where it will keep for
several weeks.

Juniper butter

Makes 150g

100g butter
50g Smoked
Butter (page
285)
6 dried juniper
berries
sea salt

Bring both types of butter to
room temperature.

Toast the juniper berries in a
dry pan over a medium-high
heat for 2 minutes. Chop very
finely or grind in a mortar.
Mix with the butters and
season with salt.

Store in the fridge for up
to 1 month.

Charcoal cream

Makes 500g

birch log
400ml double
   cream
½ teaspoon sea
   salt, or to taste
100ml 12% ättika
   (page 288) or
   3 tablespoons
   24% ättika

Set a medium-sized birch log on the fire and leave to burn until it is a solid ember.

Pour the cream into a heatproof container and add the burning ember. Cover with a lid or foil and set aside at room temperature for 1–2 hours.

Strain the cream through a fine sieve. Season with salt. Add the ättika and mix into the cream, stirring as little as possible. Chill for 1 hour until the cream thickens, then stir again to a smooth consistency.

Charcoal cream can be kept in the fridge for 5 days.

Stock syrup

Makes 1 litre

500g granulated
   sugar

Combine the sugar and 500ml water in a saucepan and bring to the boil over a medium-high heat, whisking to dissolve the sugar.

The syrup can be kept in the fridge for 1 month.

Vanilla crème pâtissière

Makes 700g

5 egg yolks
100g caster sugar
2 tablespoons
   cornflour
250ml milk
250ml cream
1 vanilla pod, split
   open

Mix together the egg yolks, sugar and cornflour in a bowl. Whisk until the sugar has dissolved.

Pour the milk and cream into a saucepan, add the vanilla pod and bring to the boil over a medium heat. Remove from the heat.

While whisking the egg mixture, pour in a third of the hot milk and cream. Keep whisking for 1–2 minutes to prevent the egg from curdling. Pour this mixture back into the milk and cream in the pan and stir to mix.

Return to the heat and stir until the cream has thickened, then simmer for 5 minutes, stirring constantly. Transfer to a bowl and leave to cool. Cover the surface of the crème with cling film to prevent a skin from forming, then keep in the fridge. Before using, remove the vanilla pod and whisk the crème pâtissière until smooth.

Grilled apple purée

Strawberry purée

Makes 400g

Makes 1.1kg

500g eating apples
(3–4 whole
apples)
caster sugar

Rinse the apples in cold
water. Place them, stem up,
on grill grates over the fire.
Grill on both sides until soft
in the centre: check with a
skewer or a paring knife. The
skin will be black and burnt.

Remove from the heat
and leave to cool down to
room temperature.

Remove the skin and core
from the apples; keep the
skin to be used later. (The
easiest way to do this is with
your hands.)

Weigh the apple flesh
with the charred skin and
add 10 per cent of this
weight in sugar. Blitz to a
smooth paste in a blender
or food processor.

Transfer the paste to a
saucepan and simmer over a
medium-low heat to reduce
to a thick, solid purée.

1kg strawberries
100g caster sugar

Combine the berries and
sugar in a blender and blitz
until smooth. Strain through
a sieve.

Store in the fridge for 3 days
or freeze.

Almond paste

Makes 1kg

500g almonds
500g caster sugar

Bring a pan of water to the
boil, add the almonds and
blanch for 2 minutes. Drain
and cool down in running
cold water. Remove the skin
from the almonds by rubbing
in a tea towel.

Combine the almonds and
sugar in a blender and blitz to
a smooth paste.

Wrap in cling film and leave
to mature for 24 hours before
using. The paste can be kept
in the fridge or freezer for
3 months.

288

Almond potatoes
These are oval in shape, somewhat resembling almonds, hence the name. It is an old variety (known since the nineteenth century), which has long been grown in the northern regions of Sweden.

Ättika
Ättika is Swedish white vinegar made by mixing water with acetic acid. The percentage indicates the concentration of acetic acid, which varies according to the vinegar's use. It is traditionally used for pickled cucumber, which is often served with Swedish meatballs, and when preserving herring.
     Alternative: white vinegar

Birch syrup
The reduced sap from birch trees. The trees are tapped and their sap collected in the spring (generally mid-to-late April, about 2–3 weeks before the leaves appear on the trees). 100–130 litres of birch sap will yield about 700ml syrup, after a time-consuming and complex process.

Black garlic
Fermented, aged garlic. The garlic is kept in the dark at about 60°C for 3–4 weeks and then dried. Originally from Asia, Korea and Thailand, black garlic is now widely available in the West.

Blackcurrant leaf powder
Dried blackcurrant leaves ground to a powder.

Bovine colostrum
This is the milk a cow produces during the first days after calving. It is rich in protein, which is what gives it the ability to coagulate when heated up without the need for any kind of thickener.

Chickweed
One of the world's most common weeds. It can grow all year round, even in the middle of winter if the temperature is mild.
     Alternative: other edible weeds and wildflowers or young spinach

Cloudberries
Golden-yellow berries, rich in vitamin C, with a distinctive tart taste. They are in season August to September. Cloudberry plants grow in the wild in northern Scandinavia in the Arctic tundra boreal forest.
     Alternative: raspberries, mulberries

Dairy beef/Basque beef
Meat from retired dairy cows. It has a really rich, deep flavour and beefy aroma.

Dried seaweed
There are many different kinds of dried seaweed, often found in healthfood shops. We use varieties from the Swedish west coast or the coast of Norway, such as kelp.

Dry-aged beef fat or tallow
We use the fat from dry-aged beef for the flambadou. Pieces are cut about 3 x 3cm.

Knäckebröd (crispbread)
Traditionally, crispbreads were baked just twice a year, first following the harvest and again in the spring when frozen river waters began to flow. The crispbreads were made as round wafers with a hole in the middle so the breads could be stored on long poles hanging near the ceiling. At the restaurant we make crispbreads in square shapes once a week. (See recipe page 224.)

Lingonberries
Deeply red berries of a low-growing evergreen bush, very tart in taste and high in acidity. They are in season late summer to early autumn and can be found almost all over Sweden.
     Alternative: slightly underripe redcurrants

Meadowsweet
Sweet-scented wildflower with frothy, creamy-white flowers that grows in damp meadows. Flowers all summer.
     Alternative: marigold flowers, elderflower

Meadowsweet syrup
This syrup seasoned with meadowsweet is fresh and aromatic, reminiscent of bitter almond.

Moose heart
Alternative: deer, venison or reindeer heart

Pine needles
At Ekstedt we use both fresh and dry pine shoots and needles. Fresh pine shoots are pickled or eaten raw; dry pine needle are used for smoking.
    Alternative: spruce shoots for pickling, juniper for smoking

Preserved lemon
Lemons brined in salt for 2–4 weeks. They have a very rich aroma, and both peel and flesh can be used.

Rapeseed flower
There are two varieties of rapeseed in Sweden, which flower during May and June. The normal use for rapeseed is to press the stems for oil but the flowers are delicious to eat when in season.

Reindeer blood
Alternative: blood from game such as moose, deer or venison. Pork and goose blood will work as well.

Seaweed salad
A mixture of edible seaweed. Thicker varieties are good to cook until tender. We use a fresh mix of haricot de mer (thongweed/sea spaghetti), wakame, laitue de mer (sea lettuce), dulse, kombu breton, nori and kombu royal.

Spruce shoots
Gathered in spring, these are delicious, citrus-flavoured shoots rich in vitamin C. Eaten raw or pickled.

Swedish mustard
A semi-sweet, smooth mustard. We use Slotts (slotts.se).

Tar syrup
A semi-sweet syrup seasoned with tar. We use Spruce of Sweden (spruceofsweden.com).

Truffle seaweed
This seaweed, *Vertebrata lanosa*, looks like dark grey or brown moss and has a delicate aroma of black truffle.
    Alternative: 3 thin slices of fresh black truffle per portion

Vendace roe
The vendace is a small freshwater fish (about 10cm in length), a member of the salmon family, found in lakes in northern Europe. The roe is considered a delicacy. A close relative, also called vendace, has been found in the Lake District in the UK.

Whey
The liquid remaining after milk has been curdled and strained when making cheese, or when cultured dairy products such as yoghurt are drained. Traditional buttermilk is the liquid left over from churning butter from cream (modern buttermilk is cultured). Butter is a key ingredient at Ekstedt, and we often make our own, which means we end up with buttermilk to be used for cooking in the same ways as whey.

Yellow pea sauce
A Swedish-made soy sauce, from split yellow peas.
    Alternative: light soy sauce

Equipment

Cast-iron doughnut pan
The pan we use is 22cm in diameter with round holes that are 6–8cm in diameter.

Cast-iron pancake pan
Ours is a flat, smooth 17cm griddle pan with a thick base, suitable for use on a wood fire.

Plättjärn
Similar to the pancake pan, this has 4–7 shallow moulds 6–8cm wide. It is also known as a Scotch pancake iron.

300

NIKLAS EKSTEDT – a pioneer of Nordic gastronomy

Niklas grew up in Järpen, a small village in Jämtland in northern Sweden. Opening his debut restaurant at the age of just 21, Niklas subsequently spent stints at el Bulli before finding his Nordic roots.

Drawn to the birch woods of the Stockholm archipelago, Niklas quickly transitioned from using a grill to a cast-iron pan on open flames – laying the foundation for a new kind of fine-dining, and altering the course of the Nordic food movement. Covered in ash and soot, Niklas and his team are on a continual journey to discover, employ and evolve what was once a lost art of cooking.

When Niklas is not working at his restaurant, he loves snowboarding and surfing with his wife Katarina and two sons Vinston and John. He lives in Danderyd, outside Stockholm.

RESTAURANT EKSTEDT – the origin of new Nordic open-fire cooking

Centred on centuries-old cooking techniques, Ekstedt set a new course for the Nordic food movement when it opened in 2011.

Chefs clad in canvas aprons toil away at the flames in full view of the guests, preparing culinary delights such as reindeer baked on glowing embers with smoked ox marrow, sweetbreads cooked in hay and juniper-smoked perch.

Restaurant Ekstedt is one of the top gastronomic destinations of Sweden and has held a Michelin star since 2013.

'No electric griddle, no gas stove – only natural heat, soot, smoke and fire.'

Acknowledgements

Thank you to my project manager Thomas Eiderfors and photographer David Loftus. Also, my Sami friends Andreas Lidström and Kajsa Fjällström. Thank you all for helping me with this book.

Thank you Jon, Meg, Emily and Marie and everyone at team Absolute. Your patience with me is really extraordinary and I'm so happy that you believe in my crazy idea of analogue cooking – until the next book!

Katie Holten's Tree Alphabet

Credits
The End

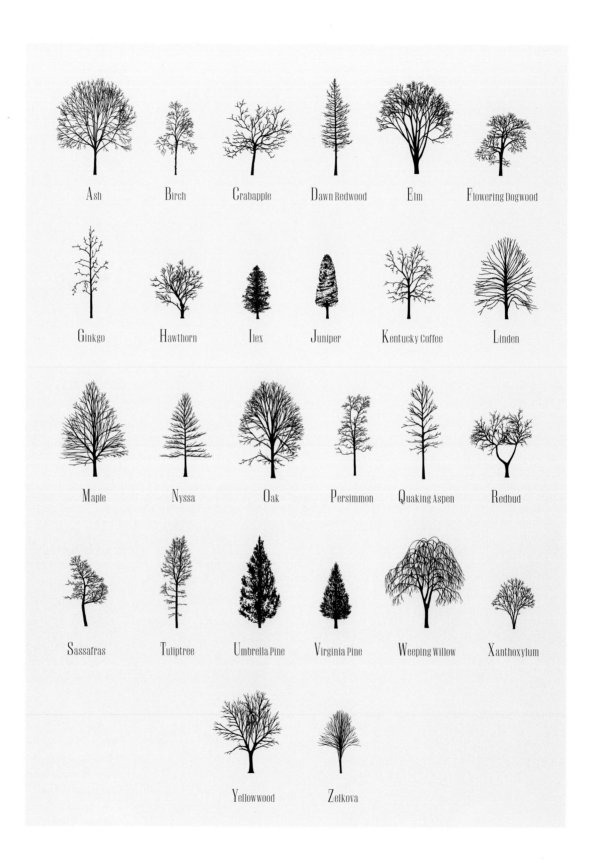

Ash   Birch   Crabapple   Dawn Redwood   Elm   Flowering Dogwood

Ginkgo   Hawthorn   Ilex   Juniper   Kentucky Coffee   Linden

Maple   Nyssa   Oak   Persimmon   Quaking Aspen   Redbud

Sassafras   Tuliptree   Umbrella Pine   Virginia Pine   Weeping Willow   Xanthoxylum

Yellowwood   Zelkova

Publisher
Jon Croft

Commissioning Editor
Meg Boas

Senior Editor
Emily North

Art Director
Marie O'Shepherd

Designers
Marie O'Shepherd and Peter Moffat

Junior Designer
Anika Schulze

Production Controller
Laura Brodie

Photography
David Loftus

Illustrator
Katie Holten

Copyeditor
Norma MacMillan

Proofreader
Margaret Haynes

Indexer
Zoe Ross

Typefaces
Set in Giorgio, Trees, Minion Pro
and Lato.
    Giorgio was created for *T, the New
York Times Style Magazine* by designer
Christian Schwartz. With strong
contrast between thick and thin and a
tall, elegant x-height it visually embodies
Ekstedt's close connection to trees.
    NYC Trees was created by Katie
Holten in 2018; at the root of Holten's
practice is a commitment to study
the inextricable relationship between
humans and nature. In 2015 she
published the book *About Tress*, offering
readers a language beyond the human.

BLOOMSBURY ABSOLUTE
Bloomsbury Publishing Plc
50 Bedford Square, London
WC1B 3DP, UK

BLOOMSBURY, BLOOMSBURY
ABSOLUTE, the Diana logo and the
Absolute Press logo are trademarks of
Bloomsbury Publishing Plc.

First published in Great Britain
in 2020.

A catalogue record for this book is available
from the British Library.

Library of Congress Cataloguing-in-
Publication data has been applied for.

HB: 9781472961969
Special Edition: 9781472978226
ePub: 9781472961976
ePDF: 9781472961952

2 4 6 8 10 9 7 5 3 1

Printed and bound in China by
C&C Offset Printing Ltd.

To find out more about our authors and
books visit www.bloomsbury.com
and sign up for our newsletters.

FSC
www.fsc.org

MIX
Paper from
responsible sources
FSC® C008047